About the Author

JOHN MCPHEE is a staff writer at *The New Yorker*.
He is the author of thirty-three books, all published
by Farrar, Straus and Giroux. He lives in Princeton,
New Jersey.

Also by John McPhee

Additional Praise for *The Patch*

"A work that gains its newness through structure alone . . . The experience of having decades of details and observations and exacting description wash over you, the time or the context of the writing never exactly clear, is a fascinating one . . . A more honest and effective way of stitching together the memories of a life, the structure in a way acknowledging that a neat beginning, middle and end is part of the artifice of writing."
—Willy Blackmore, *Los Angeles Times*

"McPhee's sentences are as varied as the geographic features he so often describes: some move at a glacial pace, some jut up unexpectedly like exposed granite, others gooseneck like snaking streams, still others burn like understory, quick, dangerous. Always his sentences capture some crystalline essence in their intricate, melodious designs—making connections, spinning webs, accreting meanings."   —Tyler Malone, *Literary Hub*

"Pulitzer winner John McPhee has spent his career covering subjects that don't inherently seem like fodder for good, much less gripping, journalism: things like geology, oranges, shad. But he's adept at making the esoteric seem essential and personal. *The Patch*, his latest collection of nonfiction essays, largely about angling and sports, is no exception . . . McPhee proves there's transcendence in the trivial and, like a good drinking pal, comes off as generous, smart, and curious about life's splendor, however small."   —J. R. Sullivan, *Men's Health*

"*The Patch*, John McPhee's new book, could only have been written by a journalist with decades of experience and an archivist's

disposition ... In McPhee's career-spanning miscellany, he marvels at Iceland's glaciers, shadows Hershey's chief chocolate taster and admires the roller-skating bears of the Moscow State Circus ... [Full of] lovely passages."
—Kevin Canfield, *Minneapolis Star Tribune*

"[McPhee] provides a bountiful cornucopia of insightful essays that display the wide range of his interests and tastes ... McPhee delights in cracking open subjects, both ordinary and esoteric, and making them accessible to the layperson in works that testify to his virtuosity as one of the greatest living American essayists."
—*Publishers Weekly* (starred review)

"Delightful ... It's a rare gift, to be able to see as well as McPhee sees, and to be given the time that it takes to describe the connections between things so clearly ... It's also rare to encounter a writer who writes so artfully about himself while hardly writing about himself at all."
—*Bookforum*

The Patch

The
Patch

John
McPhee

PICADOR   FARRAR, STRAUS AND GIROUX   NEW YORK

Picador
120 Broadway, New York 10271

Published in 2018 by Farrar, Straus and Giroux
First Picador paperback edition, November 2019

Earlier versions of most of these essays first appeared in *The New Yorker*, *Time*, and *Vogue*.

Photographs by Yolanda Whitman

The Library of Congress has cataloged the Farrar, Straus and Giroux hardcover edition as follows:
Names: McPhee, John, 1931– author.
Title: The patch / John McPhee.
Description: First edition. | New York : Farrar, Straus and Giroux, 2018. | "Earlier versions of most of these essays first appeared in The New Yorker, Time, and Vogue"—Verso title page.
Identifiers: LCCN 2018007631 | ISBN 9780374229481 (hardcover)
Classification: LCC AC8 .M267 2018 | DDC 080—dc23
LC record available at https://lccn.loc.gov/2018007631

Picador Paperback ISBN: 978-1-250-23488-9

Designed by Richard Oriolo

Our books may be purchased in bulk for promotional, educational, or business use. Please contact your local bookseller or the Macmillan Corporate and Premium Sales Department at 1-800-221-7945, extension 5442, or by e-mail at MacmillanSpecialMarkets@macmillan.com.

Picador® is a U.S. registered trademark and is used by Macmillan Publishing Group, LLC, under license from Pan Books Limited.

picadorusa.com • instagram.com/picador
twitter.com/picadorusa • facebook.com/picadorusa

For book club information, please visit facebook.com/picadorbookclub or e-mail marketing@picadorusa.com.

10 9 8 7 6 5 4 3 2 1

FOR MY GRANDCHILDREN
Ayane
Isobel
Jasper
Leandro
Livia
Nicholas
Oliver
Rebecca
Riley
Tommaso

Contents

Part I

The

Sporting

Scene

FISHING, FOOTBALL,
GOLF, LACROSSE,
AND BEARS

The Patch

YOU MOVE YOUR CANOE THROUGH OPEN WATER A FLY CAST away from a patch of lily pads. You cast just shy of the edge of the pads—inches off the edge of the pads. A chain pickerel is a lone ambush hunter. Its body resembles a barracuda's and has evolved to similar purpose. Territorial, concealed in the vegetation, it hovers; and not much but its pectoral fins are in motion. Endlessly patient, it waits for prey to come by—frogs, crayfish, newts, turtles, and smaller fish, including its own young. Long, tubular, with its pelvic fins set far back like the wings of some jets, it can accelerate like a bullet.

You lay a kiwi muddler out there—best white or yellow. In the water, it appears to be a minnow. Strip in line, more line, more line. In a swirl as audible as it is visible, the lake seems to explode. You need at least a twelve-pound leader, because this fish has teeth like concertina wire. I tried a braided steel tippet once, of a type made for fish of this family, but casting it was clunky and I gave it up in favor of monofilament thick enough to win the contest between the scissoring teeth and the time it takes to net the fish. I've been doing this for more than forty years, always in the fall in New Hampshire with my friend George Hackl, whose wife owns an undeveloped island in Lake Winnipesaukee. Chain pickerel are sluggish and indifferent in the warmer months. In the cold dawns and the cold dusks of October, they hit like hammers, some days on the surface, some days below it, a mass idiosyncrasy that is not well understood.

Thoreau understood—more than most, anyway—this "swiftest, wariest, and most ravenous of fishes . . . stately, ruminant . . . lurking under the shadow of a pad at noon . . . still, circumspect . . . motionless as a jewel set in water." He said he had "caught one which had swallowed a brother pickerel half as large as itself, with the tail still visible in its mouth," and he noted that "sometimes a striped snake, bound to greener meadows across the stream, ends its undulatory progress in the same receptacle."

Men who pass us on the lake in bass boats, sitting on their elevated seats and sweeping the water with spinning gear, are less impressed. They think of chain pickerel as trash, call them names like "slime darts," and actually laugh when we tell them what we are fishing for. They also tend to thank us. They want bass in their nets, not pickerel, and pickerel can not only outrace bass to the lures but also wreck the lures with their teeth.

We are out there neither to trash them nor admire them but to catch them for breakfast. A sautéed young pickerel is more delicious than most fish. The paradox of pickerel fishing is that a pickerel's culinary quality is in inverse proportion to its size. The big ones taste like kiln-dried basswood, and are also full of bones. The Y-shaped, intermuscular bones of the very young ones go down soft. Pickerel grow like bamboo. Ichthyologists have watched them grow an inch in two days.

As far as I know, my father never fished for chain pickerel. When I was three years old, he was the medical doctor in a summer camp on the Baie de Chaleur, and he fished for salmon in the Restigouche with his bamboo rod. He fished with grasshoppers in a Vermont gorge, and angleworms in Buzzards Bay, taking me with him when I was six, seven, eight. And across the same years, we went trout fishing in New Jersey streams. On Opening Day, in April, we would get up in the pitch dark in order to be standing beside a stream at the break of dawn. One time, as dawn broke, we discovered that the stream was frozen over. On the way home, he let me "drive." I sat in his lap and steered—seat belts an innovation not yet innovated. These are my fondest memories of my father, his best way of being close, and I therefore regret all the more that my childhood love of fishing fell away in my teen-age years, and stayed away, in favor of organized sports and other preoccupations.

The dormant angler in me remained dormant until he woke up in Arctic Alaska for the purpose of eating grayling, salmon, and char. After that, I took fishing gear on other canoe trips—down the Allagash, down the St. John—but seldom used it until the October of my forty-eighth year, camping with the Hackls on the New Hampshire island, watching the colors fall into the water, and looking around for things to do.

Sometimes when chain pickerel are hovering high they see your moving fly from a distance, and come for it, come right toward you, etching on the surface a rippling wake, like a torpedo. It takes just one such scene to arouse you forever. Across an open channel from the New Hampshire island lay a quarter mile of sharply edged lily pads, and soon we were calling it not a patch but The Patch. We scouted the lily pads of other bays, and fished every one of them, but always came back to The Patch. It was the home shore, running from a sedge fen off the tip of a neighboring island and along a white-pine forest on the mainland to the near side of another island. Our wives—Ann and Yolanda, each the other's oldest friend—were absolutely uninterested in pickerel except with their toast and coffee, but from year to year George and I grew better at fishing for them, each of us standing up and casting from his own canoe, anchored or drifting, sense of balance as yet uneroded. At the end of the seventh October, after Yolanda and I had driven home to New Jersey, we came up the driveway and the telephone inside the house was ringing as we approached the door. My brother was calling to tell me that my father was in a Baltimore County hospital, having suffered a debilitating stroke.

HIS ROOM HAD a south-facing window. My mother, in a flood of light, eighty-seven, looked even smaller than she was, and space was limited around her, with me, my brother, my sister, and a young doctor together beside the bed. I was startled by the candor of the doctor. He said the patient did not have many days to live, and he described cerebral events in language only the patient, among those present, was equipped to understand. But the patient did not understand: "He can't comprehend anything, his eyes follow nothing, he is finished," the doctor said, and we should prepare ourselves.

Wordlessly, I said to him, "You fucking bastard." My father may not have been comprehending but my mother was right there before him, and his words, like everything else in those hours, were falling upon her and dripping away like rain. Nor did he stop. There was more of the same, until he finally excused himself to continue on his rounds.

During our second day there, my mother, brother, and sister went off at one point, and I was alone for an hour in the room with my father. Eyes wide open in a fixed stare at the ceiling, he lay motionless. I wondered what to do. I wasn't about to pick up a book and read. I looked out the window for a time, at Baltimore, spilling over its beltway. I looked back at him. Spontaneously, I began to talk. In my unplanned, unprepared way, I wanted to fill the air around us with words, and keep on filling it, to no apparent purpose but, I suppose, a form of self-protection. I told him where I had been—up in New England on the lake in the canoe, casting—and that the fishing had gone well despite the cold. One day, there had been an inch of ice on the water bucket in the morning. My fingers were red as I paddled and cast. Water, coming off the fly line as I stripped it in, froze in the guides that hold the line close to the rod, and so jammed the line that it was uncastable; so I went up the rod from bottom to top punching out little disks of ice with my thumb until I could make another cast and watch a fresh torpedo come out of the vegetation.

I went on in this manner, impulsively blurting out everything I could think of about the species, now and again making comparisons and asking him questions—did he remember the sand sharks off Sias Point? the rainbows of Ripton? the bullhead he gutted beside Stony Brook that flipped out of his hand and, completely gutless, swam away?—to which I expected no answers, and got none.

WITH THOSE MINUTELY OSCILLATING FINS, a pickerel treads water in much the way that a hummingbird treads air. If the pickerel bursts forth to go after prey, it returns to the place it started from, with or without the prey. If a pickerel swirls for your fly and misses, it goes back to the exact spot from which it struck. You can return half an hour later and it will be there. You can return at the end of the day and it will be there. You can go back next year and it will be there.

In an acreage of lily pads, their territorial haunts are not always far apart. I have laid a fly on the water and seen three wakes converge upon it. Where Genio C. Scott, in *Fishing in American Waters* (1869), describes chain pickerel at such a moment, he says, "You will find cause for surprise that will force you to ejaculate." For my part, I'll admit, I damned near fell out of the canoe. An acreage of lily pads is not entirely like a woven mat. There are open spots, small clear basins, like blue gaps among clouds. By no means all the pickerel in The Patch are close to the edge as if looking out from beneath a marquee. They are also back among the gaps, and some are in acute shallows very close to shore, in case a mouse slips on something and falls into the water. To fly-cast among the gaps is much more difficult than along the edge of open water. Typically you are trying to drop a long throw into six square feet of clear space, and if you miss you will be stuck fast to nymphaeaceous stems and cursing. Yanking on your line, you will bomb the territory and retrieve a pound of weed.

This family—*Esocidae*—is not popular with aesthetes, with people who torture trout. Put a pickerel in a pond full of trout, and before long all that's in there is a larger pickerel. There are people who hunt pickerel with shotguns. In Vermont, that is legal. Two other members of the family—pike and muskellunge— are quite similar in pattern, configuration, color, and appetite, but are, of course, much and very much larger. Under each eye, chain pickerel have a black vertical bar, not unlike the black horizontal bars that are painted under the eyes of football players, and evidently for the same reason, to sharpen vision by cutting down glare. A pickerel's back is forest green, and its sides shade into a light gold that is overprinted with a black pattern of chain links as consistent and uniform as a fence. This artistic presentation is entirely in the scales, which are extremely thin and small. On a filleting board, a couple of passes with a scaler completely destroy the art, revealing plain silver skin.

On the filleting board, evidence is forthcoming that chain pickerel are as voracious as insurance companies, as greedy as banks. The stomachs, usually, are packed and distended. A well-fed pickerel will readily strike, the fact notwithstanding that it already has in its stomach a frog, say, and a crayfish and a young pickerel, each in a different stage of decomposition. I have almost never opened a pickerel and found an empty stomach. I have caught pickerel, slit their stomachs, and watched crayfish walk out undamaged. I put the crayfish back in the lake. Stomachs of pickerel have contained birds.

Pickerel have palatal teeth. They also have teeth on their tongues, not to mention those razor jaws. On their bodies, they sometimes bear scars from the teeth of other pickerel. Pickerel that have been found in the stomachs of pickerel have in turn contained pickerel in their stomachs. A minnow found in the stomach of a pickerel had a pickerel in its stomach that had in its stomach a minnow. Young pickerel start eating one another when they are scarcely two inches long. How did I know all this that was tumbling out? I was mining a preoccupation. I am the owner of not one but two copies of *An Annotated Bibliography of the Chain Pickerel*, E. J. Crossman and G. E. Lewis, the Royal Ontario Museum, 1973.

In uncounted millions, they live in the lakes, ponds, streams, and rivers of the Atlantic watershed from the Canadian Maritimes to the whole of Florida, and across to the Mississippi, and up it to the Current River in southern Missouri. They seem about as endangered as mosquitoes. In Midwestern states and elsewhere, walleyes are often called pickerel and sometimes walleyed pike. A walleye is not a pickerel, nor is it a pike; it's a perch. A bluegill maneuvers better than most fish do. Blue sharks and tunas are ultimate cruisers. In the department of acceleration— the drag race of the deep—almost nothing comes near a pike, pickerel, or muskellunge. A pickerel's body is sixty per cent muscle. Undulations move along the body in propulsive waves that culminate, like oar sculling, in straight-line forward thrust. A particularly successful tuna will catch about fifteen per cent of the fish it goes after. A trout catches half the fish it strikes at. A chain pickerel, on a good day, nails eighty per cent. The last time a frog escaped a pickerel must have been in Pliocene time.

THE YOUNG DOCTOR RETURNED, twenty-four hours exactly after his earlier visit. He touched the patient with fingers and steel, and qualified for compensation. He said there had been no change and not to expect any; the patient's comprehension would not improve. He went on as he had the day before. My father, across the years, had always seemed incapable of speaking critically of another doctor, perhaps, in a paradoxical way, because he had been present in an operating room where the mistake of another doctor had ended his mother's life. Even-tempered as he generally appeared to be, my father could blow his top, and I wondered, with respect to his profession, to what extent this situation would be testing him if he were able to listen, comprehend, and speak. Silent myself now, in the attending physician's presence, I looked down at my father in his frozen state, eighty-nine, a three-season athlete who grew up in the central neighborhoods of Youngstown, Ohio, and played football at Oberlin in a game that was won by Ohio State 128–0, captained basketball, was trained at Western Reserve, went into sports medicine for five years at Iowa State and thirty-six at Princeton, and was the head physician of U.S. Olympic teams in Helsinki, Rome, Tokyo, Innsbruck, and elsewhere. The young doctor departed.

In a small open pool in the vegetation, about halfway down The Patch, there had been, this year and last, a chain pickerel that was either too smart or too inept to get itself around an assemblage of deer hair, rabbit fur, turkey quill, marabou silk, and sharp heavy wire. The swirls had been violent every time, the strike consistently missing or spurning the fly, and coming always from the same place on the same side of the same blue gap. In the repetitive geometries of The Patch, with its paisley patterns in six acres of closed and open space, how did I know it was the same gap? I just knew, that's all. It's like running a trapline. You don't forget where the traps are; or you don't run a trapline. This gap in the lily pads was thirty yards off the mainland shore between the second-tallest white pine and a granitic outcrop projecting from Ann's island. As I was getting back into the story, again speaking aloud in the renewed privacy of the hospital room, I mentioned that I had been fishing The Patch that last morning with my father's bamboo rod, and it felt a bit heavy in the hand, but since the day he had turned it over to me I had taken it with my other rods on fishing trips, and had used it, on occasion, to keep it active because it was his. Now—just a couple of days ago—time was more than close to running out. Yolanda was calling from the island: "John, we must go! John, stop fishing! John!" It was time to load the canoe and paddle west around some islands to the car, time to depart for home, yes; but I meant to have one more drift through The Patch. From the northwest, a light breeze was coming down over the sedge fen. I called to Yolanda that I'd "be right there," then swept the bow around and headed for the fen. Since I had failed and failed again while anchored near that fish, I would let the light breeze carry me this time, freelance, free-form, moving down The Patch like the slow shadow of a cloud. Which is just what happened—a quiet slide, the light rustle on the hull, Yolanda calling twice more before she gave up. Two touches with the paddle were all that was needed to perfect the aim. Standing now, closing in, I waved the bamboo rod like a semaphore—backcasting once, twice—and then threw the line. Dropping a little short, the muddler landed on the near side of the gap. The pickerel scored the surface in crossing it, swirled, made a solid hit, and took the tight line down, wrapping it around the stems of the plants.

"I pulled him out of there plants and all," I said. "I caught him with your bamboo rod."

I looked closely at my father. His eyes had welled over. His face was damp. Six weeks later, he was dead.

Phi Beta
Football

AT A RECEPTION IN CASTINE, MAINE, YEARS AGO, I WAS
introduced to and then left alone with Dick MacPherson,
who at the time was the head coach of the New England Patriots. I had no idea what to say. What on earth could I possibly
say to the coach of the New England Patriots? Then, out of
somewhere, I remembered that Dick MacPherson was born
and raised in Old Town, Maine, on the Penobscot River, next
door to the University of Maine, in Orono. When I was seven,
eight, nine years old, in Princeton, New Jersey, our next-door
neighbor was Tad Wieman, Princeton's football coach, who

went on to become the athletic director at the University of Maine.

So I said to Dick MacPherson, "You must have known Tad Wieman."

Responding in a split second, he said, "Unbalanced line. Unbalanced mind."

In the mid-twentieth century, Princeton football hung on to a fossil offense called single wing while most college teams were mating the quarterback to the center of the line in the formation called "T." Tad Wieman's single wing was pure power football. The center was not in the center. One side was overloaded, and, with certain exceptions, you battered that side.

I acquired some of this knowledge at an early age by osmosis. Not only were Wieman and his family next door but my father, an M.D., was the football team's doctor. Margaret Wieman, the coach's wife, was a close friend of my mother. In the fall in Palmer Stadium, the two of them attended every home game in a fifty-yard-line box over a vomitorium. I was six or seven when they took me with them for the first time. I sat between my mother and Mrs. Wieman. On each play, offense and defense, Mrs. Wieman screamed. It began low. As a play developed, it crescendoed. Before runner and tackler came together, it had become a major shriek, which abruptly stopped as the play ended. Bronco Van Lengen took the snap from center, followed his blockers on a sweep, and before he was halfway around, Mrs. Wieman's voice was curdling blood. And that was my basic introduction to football.

Aged eight, I was promoted to a position on the field. Actually, I was with the college players on various fields all week long. I was in grade school in what is now a university building, and every fall day after soccer I went down the street to university football practice and hung around my father, the trainers, the student managers, the coaches, the team. A football jersey—black with orange tiger stripes on the sleeves, the number 33 front and back—was made for me by the same company that made the big guys' uniforms. On Saturdays, I went down a slanting tunnel with the team and onto the playing field in Palmer Stadium. After they scored—and in those days they really scored—I went behind the goalpost and caught the extra point.

There were indelible moments. Bronco Van Lengen goes off tackle at the closed end of the horseshoe and a great cheer rises, but Bronco is lying on the grass and not getting up. It looks so serious that not only the head trainer but my father as well hurry to the scene and kneel beside Bronco's unstirring body. Bronco opens one eye. He sees the teams collected on the one-yard line and waiting to resume play. He says, "Didn't I score?" Actually, not that time, Bronco. Bronco leaps up off the grass, adjusts his helmet, and joins the huddle.

Wieman won four straight against Yale in those years. Before one Yale game, he collected his team and unfurled before them a banner large enough to cover ten guys at once, or so it seemed to me. The banner was black with orange block letters a foot and a half high that said "PRINCETON." Speaking quietly, Wieman told his cloistered team that the banner represented what they were about to do, and nothing they had ever done was more important. Before then, I had never witnessed such a solemn scene. Wieman, of course, was not alone in this genre of forensic coaching. And a decade later, Herman Hickman, of Yale, was said to up the ante, telling his players that representing Yale on the football field would forever be the pinnacle of their lives.

■ ■ ■

BEFORE MY FATHER played football at Oberlin, class of 1917, he was winning varsity letters at Rayen High School, in Youngstown. Contemplating one of those letters, he cut the leg off the "R." He had never been east of western Pennsylvania but had nonetheless developed a mystical sense of Princeton, whose athletes were national gods during his high-school years. Later, as a doctor, he worked first at Iowa State but soon found his career post at Princeton. The younger of my father's two brothers had the same names I have, first and last. He was my Uncle Jack. He was the executive secretary of the Youngstown Y and later sold industrial lubricants to the steel industry, but on weekends he was a football official. It was Uncle Jack who threw the first flag in big-time football. Ordinarily a field judge or head linesman, he was in this instance refereeing a game at Ohio State. Officials used to carry wee horns strapped to their wrists. On observing an infraction—anywhere on the scale from offside to unnecessary roughness—they blew the horns, and that was their penalty signal for more than fifty years. Uncle Jack had been there, blown that, and in Ohio Stadium he had experienced louder, more continuous dins than he ever would in any steel plant. Much of the time, no one on the field could hear the wee horns. At the suggestion of his friend Dwight Beede, the coach of Youngstown College, Uncle Jack took a red-and-white bandanna to Columbus and instead of blowing the horn whipped the bandanna out of his pocket and dropped it on the ground. The idea had arisen here and there across the years, but now its time had come. John Griffith, the conference commissioner, instructed all Big Ten officials to show up at all Big Ten games with flags in their pockets the following week.

Before that, when I was a child, Uncle Jack had been an Eastern College Athletic Conference official, and his work included games in what is now the Ivy League. In the locker room before my first of those games—when I was with the team and about to go onto the field—my father leaned down and said to me, in a low steely voice, "Remember: do not talk to or even recognize your Uncle Jack." I had long since been taught that Uncle Jack—head linesman, in black-and-white stripes—was an official officially impartial.

Down the tunnel we went and out onto the stadium field. I saw the officials clustered near the fifty-yard line. I have never suffered from oppositional defiant disorder. Pure excitement stripped me of restraint, and in my orange-and-black tiger-striped jersey I shouted, "Uncle Jack! Uncle Jack! Uncle Jack!"

A year or two later, on a November Saturday of cold, wind-driven rain—when I was about ten—I was miserable on the stadium sidelines. The rain stung my eyes, and I was shivering. Looking up at the press box, where I knew there were space heaters, I saw those people sitting dry under a roof, and decided then and there to become a writer.

IN FOLLOWING YEARS, I did not play football, but in one way or another it continued to be close around me. One of my college roommates won the Heisman Trophy. Another played safety, catching punts and getting crushed in the absence of the fair-catch rule. A third—an English major like me—was the quarterback. Their coach was Charlie Caldwell, and the team was undefeated two straight years. One day on the campus, I happened to encounter the coach, and he told me he was writing a book—on football, what else, although it could have been baseball (he had pitched three games for the New York Yankees and had coached Princeton baseball for two seasons). He said he was having difficulty finding a title for the football book and asked me to help him, adding, "If you come up with something good, I'll give you a nice piece of change." I went away thinking, mostly about the piece of change. A week later, I suggested that he call his book *Phi Beta Football*. He called it *Modern Single Wing Football*.

One of my cousins (who was also a college classmate) was an All-American end in two of his three eligible years. Freshmen had their own teams then. Some of us played freshman basketball. Our coach was Eddie Donovan, a former Holy Cross athlete, who also coached Princeton baseball and J.V. football. Even in his fifties and sixties, Eddie Donovan seemed to be the best all-around athlete who had ever set foot on the Princeton campus, whether he was hitting his precision fungoes, outshooting Bill Bradley at h-o-r-s-e, or besting various champions in squash, tennis, and golf. He took his J.V. football team to Maryland when the Maryland varsity was among the highest-ranked nationally. Right from the kickoff, Donovan's J.V.'s outscored the Maryland J.V.'s and pushed them all over College Park. In the second half, things changed. Maryland scored, scored again, scored again. Sending in a substitute, Donovan said to the player coming off the field, "What is going on out there?" The player said, "Coach, those are the same uniforms but different guys."

The varsity quarterback I mentioned was George Stevens, who went on to be headmaster of New Canaan Country School. The punt-catching safety was John McGillicuddy, who became the C.E.O. of Manufacturers Hanover Trust and eventually merged it with Chemical Bank. His high-school field in Harrison, New York, is named for him. The Heisman winner was Dick Kazmaier, who went to Harvard Business School instead of the N.F.L. All three are no longer alive. There were ten of us around a central living room, where a sign on a wall asked what it might have been like to be a college roommate of Red Grange. As I said in an introduction at an event some fifty years later, we knew what it was like to live with Dick. He had better things to do than play gin rummy. He drew a tight circle around his teammates, roommates, and other friends. Across the years, he often said that what mattered to him most at Princeton was, in his words, "what I was part of: I was like every other student." He alluded to the Heisman Trophy and all that went with it as "an unusual external part of the picture."

He was enduringly superstitious. When he went down the tunnel into Palmer Stadium for football games, he was always the last player. It had been so augured. Somewhere. He told George the quarterback never to let him touch the ball on Princeton's first play. In the old single wing, the tailback and the fullback always lined up where either one could take the snap. Dick was the tailback, Russ McNeil the fullback. After other teams somehow became aware of Kazmaier's superstition, Russ McNeil, on the first play, went down like General Custer. The number that Kazmaier wore—42—became his lucky number. His Massachusetts license plate was KA42. His e-mail address was RWK4252@earthlink.net ('52 being his class year). When he was in a restaurant, if the check came to x dollars and forty-two cents he was made happier than he could ever be by the sum contents of ten thousand fortune cookies. Seat number 42 in any kind of theatre or arena was a good-luck seat. His company, Kazmaier Associates, on Elm Street, in Concord, Massachusetts, seemed to have a tentacle in every aspect of most known sports, from the international licensing of basketball broadcasts to the manufacture and sale of baseball uniforms and football helmets. Dick's parking space at Kazmaier Associates was No. 42. There were thirty-six spaces in the parking lot.

THOSE OF US who are still around are in our eighties now. For a decade or so, I have been back on Princeton sidelines in the sorcerous capacity of Faculty Fellow of Men's Lacrosse. This has not passed unnoticed by my daughters, least of all the youngest, Martha, who also teaches writing in a college (Hofstra) but does not haunt the stadium there. Recently, after listening to one of my game summaries over the telephone, Martha said, "Dad, when you were eight years old, you were a mascot on the sidelines at Princeton, and you're a mascot on the Princeton sidelines now."

Bill Belichick has come to Princeton with the Johns Hopkins men's lacrosse team. Belichick loves lacrosse. He once warmed up a Hopkins goalie. The fact that recent N.C.A.A. final fours in college lacrosse have been held in the N.F.L. stadium in Foxborough, Massachusetts, owes itself to the fact that he coaches there. He grew up in Annapolis, Maryland, where lacrosse goals are in people's yards and lacrosse has more status than football. He played lacrosse for Annapolis High School, and in a PG year at Andover. He played at Wesleyan. His children are lacrosse players. I have not had the moxie even to think of approaching him. What on earth could I possibly say to the coach of the New England Patriots?

Early in the season, Princeton football practices often occurred in high heat. Not to mention humidity. Charging, blocking, punting, grunting, everybody dehydrated by the quart. My otherwise benevolent father forbad them to drink ordinary water. They were losing electrolytes, and they needed to hydrate and electrolyze. Buckets beside the practice fields held the only fluid my father would allow the players to drink. They complained. They further complained. But they were so thirsty that they dipped ladles into the buckets and drank. The fluid tasted awful, as I can testify, because—age eight, age nine— I drank it, too. It was an aqueous solution of sodium chloride, sodium phosphate, and potassium chloride. Why am I telling this story? Because, twenty years later, researchers at the University of Florida College of Medicine, responding to a request from Coach Ray Graves, developed a drink full of electrolytes to hydrolyze the Florida Gators. The difference between Gatorade and the solution in my father's buckets was sugar and fruit flavoring—healthless components that were evidently of no interest to my father or I would be writing this from one of my seasonal villas.

The
Orange
Trapper

FISHING FROM A CANOE IN THE DELAWARE RIVER, I LIKE
to ship the paddle and let the boat go where it will. I watch
the stony bottom, which flies by under fast-moving water. This
is not Philadelphia. This is two hundred river miles above Philadelphia, where the stream-rounded rocks are so clear they look
printed. Shoving the rocks, anadromous lampreys have built
fortress nests, which are spread around the river like craters of
the moon. Mesmerized, I watch the rocks go by. Fly-casting for
bass, I see golf balls.

From shallows in the Merrimack in Manchester, New

Hampshire, I once picked up a ball that bore the logo of a country club two and a half miles upstream. If the river brought it there, the ball had come through deep water and then over the Amoskeag Dam. In the Connecticut River above Northampton, Massachusetts, I've seen golf balls by the constellation—too deep to reach and too far from any upstream golf course for their presence to make sense unless people hit them off their lawns. Compulsions are easy to come by and hard to explain. Mine include watching for golf balls, which I do with acute attention, the fact notwithstanding that I quit golf cold when I was twenty-four. These days, my principal form of exercise is on a bicycle, which I ride a good bit upwards of two thousand miles a year. I go past golf courses. How could I not? I live in New Jersey, which has a golf-course density of five per hundred square miles, or twice the G.C.D. of Florida, which has more golf courses than any other state. Moreover, the vast undeveloped forests of the southern part of New Jersey tend to shove the densities toward and beyond Princeton, in whose environs I ride my bike. The woods that lie between public roads and private fairways remind me of the dry terrain between a river levee and the river itself. In Louisiana along the Mississippi this isolated and often wooded space is known as the river batture. If you're in Louisiana, you pronounce it "batcher." From my bicycle in New Jersey, if I am passing a golf-links batture, my head is turned that way and my gaze runs through the woods until a white dot stops it, which is not an infrequent occurrence. I get off my bike and collect the ball.

The Delaware is less accommodating. When you are flying along on fast current, you don't just get off your canoe and prop it up on a kickstand in order to pick up a golf ball. Over time, seeing so many golf balls in the river was such a threatening frustration that I had to do something about it. Research led to the telephone number of a company then in Michigan. A real person answered and was even more than real. She understood me. She knew what I was asking and did not call 911. Instead, she had questions of her own: What was the speed of the current? What was the depth of the river? Was the bottom free-stone? Sand? Clay? Silt? After completing the interview, she said, "You want the Orange Trapper."

"The Orange Trapper?"

"The Orange Trapper."

It came in various lengths. I said I thought the nine-footer would do. The nine might be stiffer in the current than the twelve, fifteen, eighteen, twenty-one, or twenty-four. Besides, nine (actually 9.6) just felt right. It was the length of my fly rods.

What came in the mail was only twenty-one inches long, with an orange head, a black grip, and a telescoping shaft that consisted of ten concentric stainless tubes with a maximum diameter of five-eighths of an inch. You could conduct an orchestra with it. It was beautiful. The orange head was a band of industrial-strength plastic, as obovate as a pear and slightly wider than a golf ball. A depression in its inside top was there to secure one side of a ball, but the genius of the device was in a working part, a bevelled "flipper" that came up through the throat and would waggle into place on the other side of the ball. The Orange Trapper worked two ways. It had no upside or downside. You could surround a golf ball with either side, then lift it up as if you were playing lacrosse with no strings. You could turn the head over—a hundred and eighty degrees—and the ball would generally stay put. But flip the thing over once more and the ball would always roll free. Made by JTD Enterprises, it could have been designed by Apple.

Even so, finesse was required to trap a ball in shallow current. After seeing one, and swinging around, and going hard upstream, and shipping the paddle, you had about five seconds to place the head of the Trapper over the ball. I missed as often as not. It wasn't the Trapper's fault. My average would have been higher chasing hummingbirds with a butterfly net. The river is an almost endless sequence of shallows, riffles, rapids, and slow pools. For the real action, I went below some white water into a long deep pool with Don Schlaefer in his johnboat. Don is a fishing pal. He plays golf. He had no interest in the balls in the river, but he could put his boat right over them and hold it there while I fished with the Orange Trapper. I picked up a dozen golf balls in half an hour.

Marvelling at the craziness, Don said, "Why are you doing this? They're only golf balls. Golf balls are cheap."

I said, "Money has nothing to do with it."

A Titleist Pro V1, currently the Prada golf ball, costs four or five dollars on the Internet and more in a pro shop. If a person of Scottish blood says money has nothing to do with that, he is really around the corner. True, I don't find balls of such quality often in the river. But they're a high percentage of what I pick up in the roadside woods of New Jersey. Titleist makes about a million balls a day. In the United States, for all qualities and brands, a present estimate is that golfers lose three hundred million golf balls a year.

Why? Ask George Hackl, who grew up playing golf on courses around Princeton, now lives in central New Hampshire, and is a member of Bald Peak, Yeamans Hall, Pine Valley, and the Royal and Ancient Golf Club of St. Andrews.

Hackl: "It is an indication of the vast disparity of wealth in this country that golfers in some places can hit seven-dollar balls into woods and thickets and not even bother to look for them."

There is less to it than that. Golfers have egos in the surgeon range. They hit a drive, miss the fairway, and go looking for the ball thirty yards past where it landed. When their next drive goes into timber and sounds like a woodpecker in the trees, there is no way to know the vector of the carom, so they drop another ball and play on. It must be said, in their defense, that various pressures concatenate and force them to keep moving, no matter the cost in golf balls. The foursome behind is impatient. A major issue is how long it takes to play. It is infra dig to cause "undue delay." In the Rules of Golf, there's a five-minute time limit on looking for lost balls. The rule may be unknown to some golfers and by others ignored, but five minutes or less is what most golfers give to finding lost balls. The rest are mine.

YOU GET OFF YOUR BIKE, pick up a ball, and sometimes are able to identify the species it hit. Pine pitch makes a clear impression. Tulip poplars tend to smear. An oak or hickory leaves a signature writ small and simple. A maple does not leave maple syrup. At your kitchen sink, you can tell how long a ball sat on the ground by the length of time required to take the ground off the ball.

With felt-tip pens and indelible ink, golfers decorate balls to individualize them beyond the markings of the manufacturer. If more than one player is using a Callaway 3 HX HOT BITE or a Pinnacle 4 GOLD FX LONG—or, far more commonly, there's a coincidence of Titleists—you need your own pine tree. Some golfers' graffiti are so elaborate that they resemble spiderwebs festooned with Christmas ornaments. Golfers also draw straight, longitudinal lines that serve as gunsights in putting. It is possible to mark a ball with a ballpoint pen, but some golfers actually believe that the weight of ballpoint ink, altering the pattern of flight, will affect the precision of their shots. It is tempting to say that the prevalence of this belief is in direct proportion to handicap.

In the frenzy of marketing, golf balls are sold in such complex variety that golf's pro shops are not far behind fishing's fly shops, where line weights and rod weights and tip flex and reel seats are sold in so many forms for so many different capabilities and so many different situations that people's basements are forested with tackle. And, as with fishing equipment, the spectrum of subtlety in golf balls includes price. The difference is not among manufacturers but within the product lines of manufacturers. You can buy a dozen Titleist DT SoLos for less than twenty dollars. I know a golfer who has spoken as follows about looking for a wayward ball: "If you don't find yours but find another of the same quality, you're even. If you find a ball that's not up to your standards, you leave it there for a lower class of golfer." How he happened to get into the woods in the first place was not a topic he addressed. He reminded me of a pirate in the Guayas River near Guayaquil. With six other pirates, he came off a needle boat and over the stern of a Lykes Brothers merchant ship. They were armed mainly with knives. One of them held a hacksaw blade at a sailor's throat while others tied him to a king post. A pirate pointed at the sailor's watch and said, "Give me." The sailor handed over the watch. The pirate looked at it and gave it back.

There's more to decode on a lost ball than someone's subjective hieroglyph. One Easter Sunday in Princeton, I picked up a Titleist Pro V1x that was so far off the nearest fairway it was almost in the street. On one side of the ball, a logo in very small red block letters said "CORNELL UNIVERSITY." I went home and looked up the schedule of the Princeton golf team. On Good Friday and Black Saturday, fourteen schools had competed in the Princeton Invitational Tournament. As that ball suggested, the order of finish was 1 Rutgers, 2 Yale, 3 Penn, 4 Columbia, 5 St. Bonaventure, 6 St. John's, 7 Princeton, 8 Harvard, 9 Towson, 10 Connecticut and George Mason (tied), 12 St. Joseph's, 13 Rider, and 14 Cornell.

The course, called Springdale, is on land owned by Princeton University and leased to a private club. It has been there since 1902, and in the heraldry on its lost balls you can see who plays there now.

> Titleist 2 NXT Extreme Ivy Funds
> Titleist 2 Pro V1 392 CHUBB
> Titleist 3 Pro V1 392 Morgan Stanley Funds
> Titleist 4 DT 90 The Pasadena Group of Mutual Funds
> Titleist 1 DT SoLo CREDIT SUISSE/FIRST BOSTON
> Titleist 2 Bowne Financial
> Titleist 3 Pro V1 392 STATE FARM
> Titleist 4 AIG AMERICAN GENERAL
> Titleist 3 NXT-Tour ASSURANT
> Titleist 3 Pro V1x BOLI (Bank-Owned Life Insurance)
> Titleist 4 Pro V1 MFS INVESTMENT
>   MANAGEMENT
> Top-Flite 1 XL 3000 Super Long MAXIMUM
>   INVESTMENTS
> Top-Flite 1 XL 2000 Extra Long New Jersey Lottery

That modest sample was gathered in a wooded batture on the slice side of one par-4 hole—off the course and out of bounds. Recently, I was on a ride with Griff Witte, of *The Washington Post*, who was in Princeton to teach a course in the same writing program I teach in, and we spotted eighteen essentially new golf balls in that same copse, all within ten feet of the curb. There is something Einsteinian about that patch of woods, as if the Institute for Advanced Study, which is across the street, is experimentally affecting the trajectories of tee shots and approach shots, bending light.

Of course, the golfers who play there are not all wealth manipulators.

Callaway 3 HX DIABLO TOUR New York City
  Physicians Golfing Association logo with the rod of
  Asclepius and two irons
Pinnacle 1 Extreme XOMED Surgical Products, green
  and blue
Titleist 2 VELOCITY Urologic Consultants
Nike 3 SUPER FAR with escutcheon of CHIEF,
  Burlington County Chiefs of Police Association
Titleist 4 Pro V1x 332 AJGA (American Junior Golf
  Association)
Nike 1 ONEGOLD IJGT (International Junior Golf
  Tour)
Titleist 4 EMERSON Climate Technologies
Titleist 1 384 DT 90 CALGON Carbon Corporation
two Titleists Stone & Webster engineering
three Nike DISTANCE, each with the logo of *Golf
  Magazine* (three editors, all errant? or one editor who
  hit three awful shots?)

And whoever the golfers may be, they seem to be jet-set cosmopolitan.

Pinnacle 1 Power Core MAUNA LANI
Titleist 4 NXT MAUNA KEA
Titleist GSE, orange-and-green logo, HONG KONG
Medalist 1 Acushnet THE ROLLS OF MONMOUTH,
the logo a human hand holding a scroll within a swirling
green "R" that more or less resembles a golf swing.
Internet: "The Rolls of Monmouth Golf Club, with its
championship 6,733 yard golf course, is set in superb
countryside with spectacular views of the Welsh hills.
It is one of the most outstanding golf courses, not just in
Wales, but in the whole of the UK."

That is a far cry from what was lying around this course during the Second World War. I was a caddie here, spending a lot of time looking for balls hit away by lumber dealers and local doctors. Rubber had gone to war, and after Pearl Harbor golf balls manufactured before the war became ever more scarce with the passage of time. Hunting them was not just part of work and play; it was a treasure hunt, off the charts above Easter eggs and into fraternity with the Eustace diamonds. The pro and the greenkeeper colluded in collecting them and selling them to the golfers, so in combing the woods in one's own interest there was adrenalizing stealth and insubordination. No potential threat was ever going to stop me if I came upon a golf ball lost and abandoned, and apparently nothing ever will.

There was something we called a war ball. It was made with a synthetic that shared few, if any, characteristics with latex. It shared many characteristics with granite gneiss. When you hit it hard and square, the nerve ends in your arms were outraged and the ball moved forward a short distance. My father used war balls. They didn't cost him much, because he hit them straight, didn't lose them, and would never have dreamed of throwing them away. He was a medical doctor but he wore kilts in variety shows when he impersonated Harry Lauder. Four years after the war ended, he was playing a Kro-Flite that may not have been a war ball but looked as if it had been through a war. I was thinking of that ball when I wrote a poem about him to accompany a present I was giving him for Christmas—precisely what present, I don't remember, possibly a tee. The poem was more than thirty lines long and included these four:

He took up golf
And learned with tears,
And used one ball
For fifteen years.

On an August Wednesday in the late forties, he teed up that Kro-Flite and drove it down the twelfth at Springdale, a par 4 at 413 yards. I don't know what club he used for his second shot—probably a brassie, as the longest-distance fairway wood was known then, because a couple of hundred yards was a mile by Kro-Flite. The ball took off, avoided the woodlot that bordered the twelfth on the right, sailed past a footbridge that crossed a stream, landed on the apron, rolled onto the green, and went straight into the hole. An eagle achieved that way is a more exalted feat than a par-3 hole in one. I am looking at that Kro-Flite as I write this. Beige with age, it sits on a tee set in cedar. Preserving that ball must have created great conflict in my father, whose middle name was Roemer but might as well have been Thrift.

THE TWENTIETH CENTURY was the age of the wound golf ball. An all but endless thin rubber band was wound around a solid core and wound around and around and around, until the growing sphere was large enough to be surrounded in turn by a vulcanized cover. Some manufacturers tried steel bearings as cores. Others advertised the aerodynamic mysteries of balls with liquid centers. How a rubber band can be wrapped around a liquid seems a fair question to ask. You freeze the liquid center and let it melt inside the finished ball. There was an even fairer question: What is the liquid in the liquid center? This kept whole law firms feverish in defense of intellectual property, no matter that the supersecret ingredients were water, salt, and corn syrup, even honey.

Covers were not as tough as they are now, not nearly as protective of the ball or the ego, and the ubiquitous signature of the bad golfer was a "smile," where a ball had been cut into by a mis-hit iron. If you peeled back the cover with your penknife and then went on whittling into the rubber band, ends popped up like frizzy hair. If you whittled into a war ball, what you found inside was rock solid. Oddly, that is what golf balls look like today after you split them with a table saw. Core, mantle, crust—they are models of the very planet they are filling up at a rate worldwide approaching a billion a year.

The wound-ball era began in 1898 and ended in 2000, when Titleist introduced the Pro V1, with its solid core. This was no war ball. The synthetic polybutadiene, first polymerized in czarist Russia, had undergone a series of catalytic refinements—titanium to nickel to cobalt to neodymium—that had led to more durable flexibilities in tires and extra distance in golf balls. A generation of solid-core balls was introduced in the nineteen-seventies, but players didn't use them. The balls travelled farther but were less controllable. It was a matter of spin, and relative softness. The Spalding Top-Flite felt so hard it was called Rock-Flite.

In the first three years of the twenty-first century, average driving distances on the P.G.A. Tour went up thirteen yards. The distance was in the solid core but the control and comfort were bestowed by a new urethane cover that felt soft like a wound ball and gave players the spin they were looking for. In a display of contemporary golf balls sliced open hemispherically, we are back to geophysics. The TaylorMade Penta TP consists of five concentric spheres like old Gaia herself—crust, upper mantle, asthenosphere, lower mantle, core. There are four-piece balls and three-piece balls, not to mention the core-and-cover two-piece ball. Country-club golfers are attracted to differences that, in bogey golf, make no difference. There is even a one-piece golf ball, on which the dimples are extremities of the core. Sporting-goods empires have not been built on the one-piece ball. Some golfers, carrying technology into their own kitchens, have thought that if you heat up a golf ball it goes farther. And there is some truth in the proposition. One guy heated up his ball in his microwave. As he took it out, it blew off two of his fingers.

Golf balls are so well made now that they are said to last five hundred years, although it is not clear who would know that. Environmentalists have expressed concern about the amount of zinc in lost golf balls and what will happen when it escapes, to which golfdom responds that there is less zinc in a million golf balls than in five bottles of mouthwash. Today, as during the Second World War, there is negotiability in used golf balls. Organized companies under contract to country clubs collect them and sell them to discount stores. At TPC Sawgrass, near Jacksonville, the seventeenth green spends a lot of time on television, because it is essentially an island, connected to the rest of the course by only a narrow causeway. Year in, year out, golfers, on average, hit two hundred and seventy-four balls a day into the water around that green.

I used to give the balls I found to my shad-and-pickerel-fishing companion George Hackl—Member Hackl of St. Andrews, et cetera, who long had a single-digit handicap. In New Hampshire, snowbound, he has a barnlike basement in which he putts, chips, and even drives golf balls. On the Internet, I once bought green yard goods patterned with white golf balls and colorful tees, and my wife, Yolanda Whitman, fashioned sleeves from it which would each hold a couple of dozen balls for presentation to Hackl. But Hackl is rich and does not merit such largesse—not in Yolanda's opinion, anyway—and she brought down the hammer. No more sleeves. No more golf balls for Hackl. So I turned for help to The First Tee.

This is a national organization, headquartered in Florida, that has taught golf to millions of children, primarily in inner cities, since it was founded in 1997. The nearest chapter to my home in Princeton is The First Tee of Greater Trenton, which operates even in winter, in the Y on Pennington Avenue. Not long ago, a similar program called Swing 2 Tee was set up by Pat Lindsay-Harvey and Carol Sinkler, using the "SNAG (Start

New At Golf) equipment, instruction, and assessment system."
I give balls to them, too, usually six or seven dozen at a time, but
there was one memorable day a couple of years ago when the
number greatly exceeded that. I had informed Hackl that he had
become golfer non grata, and suggested to him that he turn over
to me some of the golf balls I had given him, and any others he
could spare. On his next trip to New Jersey, he brought me two
hundred and seven golf balls. On the same day, Bryce Chase—a
liability lawyer, golfer, and lacrosse coach who is one of my routine biking companions—inventoried his garage and turned
over to me eight hundred and thirteen balls. Not a few of them
were still in their original cardboard cartons—brand new, but
not Bryce's brand. They are given to him by well-wishers who
apparently don't know that Bryce is like a pirate on a merchant
ship spurning a sailor's watch. Thanks to Bryce Chase and George
Hackl, my single day's haul for Swing 2 Tee and The First Tee of
Greater Trenton was one thousand and twenty golf balls.

ON ONE EDGE OF PRINCETON, close to Province Line Road,
is TPC Jasna Polana, a championship golf course designed by
Gary Player. The clubhouse was once the zillion-dollar home of
Seward Johnson, a Johnson & Johnson Johnson, whose young
Polish widow, when it came to that, preferred southern Europe
to western Princeton and effected the conversion of her estate—
with its Flemish tapestries, its marble mantels, its bronze case-
ments, its flying travertine staircase, its orchid house—to golf.
Numerous memberships at Jasna Polana are corporate. Avis
is a member. Citibank. Deutsche Bank. Barclays. BlackRock
Funds. Brown Brothers Harriman. Bristol-Myers Squibb. Bank
of America Merrill Lynch.

It happens that a hiking-and-birding trail, some of it paved, runs down a stream called Stony Brook, crosses the water on a footbridge, and continues beside Jasna Polana for two or three hundred yards before intersecting U.S. 206, the road to Trenton. This is not on one of my biking routes, but on solo rides I have been there, and returned there, inspired by curiosity and a longing for variety and, not least, the observation that in the thickets and copses and wild thorny roses on the inside of Jasna Polana's chain-link fence are golf balls—Big Bank golf balls, Big Pharma golf balls, C-level golf balls (C.E.O., C.O.O., C.F.O. golf balls), lying there abandoned forever by people who are snorkeling in Caneel Bay. I couldn't help noticing that the apertures among the chain links were slightly wider than two inches. This—no less than any lake, stream, or marsh—was a situation for the Orange Trapper.

Extended full length, it bends slightly from its own weight, and quivers, wandlike, which amplifies the degree of difficulty if you have inserted it through a chain-link fence and are trying to settle the orange head around a golf ball inside a bramble of wild rose. In Sherwood Forest, R. Hood had an easier time of it. You are holding the grip with one hand, against the fence, and the head is trying to settle on the ball, nine feet into Jasna Polana. On the third or fourth try, the lowering band surrounds the ball. You raise the head, the ball rolls free. You do it all again, and raise the head. The ball rolls free. You do it all again. The flipper clicks into place. The ball is rising through the roses. Inch by inch, you bring the nine feet back through the fence, ready to try again if the flipper fails. With nearly nine feet of shaft now bobbing behind you, the trapped ball has arrived at the chain link. You pull it through, inside its orange band, as if you had experience as an obstetrician. You flip the ball into your hand—a Pro V1x with the logo of ICBA Securities (Independent Community Bankers of America). You move a few feet up the fence and go after another ball.

I was working that fence near 206 one day, where Jasna Polana has a service gate. Preoccupied by the delicacy of Trapper placement, I was slow to notice a middle-aged, heavyset greenkeeper hurrying on foot toward the gate. He was past the age of running but he was chugging flat out, and this was no place for me. I withdrew the Orange Trapper, collapsed its telescoping shaft, put it into a saddlebag with the day's harvest, jumped onto my bicycle, and headed back upstream, upwoods, and away from 206 at a speed so blazing that I probably could not duplicate it if I were to try to now, but that was years ago, when I was eighty.

Rand Jerris, who grew up in northern New Jersey and went to Williams College, was a graduate student in my writing class in 1997. He was an art historian with a lifelong passion for golf, and before long became the director of the museum and archives of the United States Golf Association, in Far Hills. Thirty miles apart, we kept up over the years, and one spring day, in 2007, he invited me to observe with him the U.S. Open Championship, at Oakmont, near Pittsburgh. I had completely quit playing golf fifty years earlier, but I went, gratefully, and with no intention of writing anything until I had been on the scene half an hour and found myself scribbling notes and more notes. Walking the course with Rand was about the same as walking the course with a golf encyclopedia—the setting and the history no less immediate than the fact that Angel Cabrera was outshooting Tiger Woods in the year that Tiger won nearly eleven million dollars on the tour. I wrote a piece calling myself Rip Van Golfer, and in a private thank-you note to Rand said, "No Rand, no Rip." Four years later, Rand mentioned St. Andrews, where he had never been, and where, in the rotational migration of the British championship, the 2010 Open would be played. If ever there was a scene where setting and history marched side by side with the current event, this was the scene, the backdrop to the victory of a young South African farmer.

Linksland
and
Bottle

WHEN CHAMPIONSHIP GOLF COURSES HAD NO GRANDSTANDS, spectators came with folding stepladders in order to see over the mass of heads blocking their view. To the U.S. Open at Winged Foot in 1929, a lady in a flapper dress and a wide-brimmed hat brought a bamboo pole and two guys, who held the pole three feet off the ground while she stood on it between them for an unimpeded view of Al Espinosa and Bobby Jones. She kept her balance by placing a hand on each porter's head.

By 1947, when I was spending the summer caddying in Wisconsin and happened to visit the All-American Open at the Tam O'Shanter Country Club in Niles, Illinois, cardboard periscopes were on sale, and I bought one. Long square columns with angled mirrors, they had become so popular that they gave the compressed galleries an agronomic look, as if they were a growing crop. Through my periscope, I watched Arthur D'Arcy (Bobby) Locke, of South Africa, in his white shoes and plus-fours, tracking long winning putts with his hickory-shafted gooseneck putter. Although I couldn't actually see him, just his twice-caromed image, he became my instant golfing hero, and he did not disappoint. He went on to win the British Open four times.

I also periscoped Ben Hogan in an early round of the U.S. Open at Merion in 1950, but not long thereafter I abandoned golf in all forms except television, and did not actually go to a tournament until the U.S. Open at Oakmont, in 2007. In the twenty-first century, this is what had become of the periscopes and the stepladders: loaned to the press was a TwitterPod sort of thing called myLeaderboard. It was tied into the United States Golf Association's central real-time scoring system. You could choose any player in the field and learn what he was doing at any time; you could store certain groups, and the device would follow them. TV screens in countless places—some of them outdoors and in size reminiscent of drive-in movies—gave spectators carrying myLeaderboard the visual assistance necessary for a complete championship experience; myLeaderboard lacked a future, however. Spectators at subsequent U.S. Opens have been commercially encouraged to carry in their hands the four-inch screens of Kangaroo TV, a Canadian company that covers many sports through various on-site feeds and "allows fans attending live events to see and hear all of the action."

And now, in 2010 at St. Andrews, on the sesquicentennial

of the British Open, no one was feeding anything to handheld TV, but neither was the technology of the spectator experience a hundred and fifty years old. For eight pounds sterling, you could buy an "on-course radio" that hung around your neck like a medal while half a dozen commentators described the action through plugs in your ears. On this hallowed Scottish golf course—the Old Course, closely surrounded by five other golf courses—the radio was something like an Acoustiguide in the Victoria and Albert Museum, with the difference that you might not be seeing what you were hearing. While—as described into your ears—a bunker shot beside the fourteenth green made a high tight parabola that stopped within a foot of the flagstick, you would be watching, say, Angel Cabrera driving on the first into the Swilken Burn. "Up and down like an Otis lift!" said Radio Free Fife, whose services were nonetheless valuable.

And pedagogical: "'British Open' is an Americanism," the radio intoned. In Great Britain, yes, it is known simply as the Open, in the way that the Oxford-Cambridge annual eight-oared crew competition is known as the Boat Race, in the way that the apex of American baseball is known as the World Series, and in the way that the revival of Jesus Christ is known as the Resurrection. From Angus to Ayrshire, Fife to Kent, the rota, as it is called, moves currently among nine golf courses. Wars had shut down the championship, and this was actually the hundred-and-thirty-ninth playing of it, the twenty-eighth at St. Andrews, and there was not a lot of dramatic tension in the 2010 Open unless you found it dramatic that a twenty-seven-year-old who had missed three cuts in recent weeks (including the cut at the U.S. Open in Pebble Beach) and ranked fifty-fourth in the world started off as a flash in the pan and then went on flashing and—on the third and fourth days, when he was supposed to go dark—flashed brighter and finished one stroke short of a record set ten years before by Tiger Woods. Leaving far behind the likes of Woods (twenty-third) and Phil Mickelson (forty-eighth), Lodewicus Theodorus Oosthuizen collected a prize of eight hundred and fifty thousand pounds and bought a tractor for his farm in the Western Cape of South Africa, where he was born.

"I won't talk to them if they call me that." He answers to Louis now.

After a visit in London, I was joined at St. Andrews before the tournament by Rand Jerris, director of communications and director of the museum and archives of the United States Golf Association, shepherd of the press and post-round interviewer of golfers at U.S. Opens, who had never been to Scotland or seen a British Open. On the evening he arrived, he was so stirred just by being there that we walked the unpopulated course from one end to the other and back in a dense and darkening fog. It is not a long walk—maybe three miles round-trip—because when golf was first played there, on the linksland beside the North Sea, the golfers, speaking Middle English, knocked the ball north to a dunish point over water, then turned around and knocked the ball south on the same path, using the same holes. Grazing animals had eaten away the secondary rough, and there were patches of open sand. The Old Course contains its original self and has evolved at less than Darwinian speed. Jerris is a living textbook of golf and golf-course architecture, and one of the first remarks he made was that he could see Augusta National in that fog. He said that Alister MacKenzie, a Boer War surgeon, English, born in Yorkshire of Scottish parents, had surveyed and mapped the Old Course in the early nineteen-twenties for the Royal and Ancient Golf Club. Having dropped surgery, MacKenzie went on to be a golf-course architect and designed, among many courses in the world, Cypress Point, Royal Melbourne, and Augusta National (with Bobby Jones). In this treeless and littoral terrain, the waters beside it did not suggest to me the Savannah River, but Jerris's concentration was on the swales, hollows, and longitudinal mounds of the fairways.

I had known Jerris since the nineteen-nineties, when he was a graduate student at Princeton. After Williams College, he had entered the Ph.D. program in geology at Duke, but had become uncomfortable in the Duke curriculum and had eventually landed in Princeton's Ph.D. program in art history. Recently I asked Lincoln Hollister, a Princeton professor of petrology, how many people he thought could bring off such a move. Hollister said, "One." Jerris wrote his dissertation on sixth-century to tenth-century churches in the Swiss valley of the Engadine. Absorbed from childhood by golf, he also did an art-history paper on golf courses and the picturesque movement in landscape architecture—golf courses fitting landscapes and not altering them. In Scotland, the natural courses come in three main forms: the linksland courses by the sea, the moorland courses everywhere, and the forested parkland courses of the interior, some involving eskers, drumlins, and lateral moraines, but all the result of various glacial effects. In the United States for almost a century land has been shaped with bulldozers to imitate those forms. After we had walked a mile, a grandstand suddenly materialized in a shroud of fog, a uniformed security guard shivering beside it. He told us to be careful if we meant to continue to the far end. The tee and green signage notwithstanding, we could get turned around and lost.

■ ■ ■

WE ALSO WALKED THE COURSE, on the second day of play, with the golf historian David Hamilton, a friend of Jerris's, who lives in St. Andrews and is a member of the R&A, as the Royal and Ancient Golf Club is known to almost everyone in the world who has ever played enough to break 120 and a scattered few who have not. Rory McIlroy, of Northern Ireland, had shot 63 on the first day, writing his name in golf history beside others' for the lowest score ever made in a major championship. (Johnny Miller's 63 at Oakmont in the 1973 U.S. Open stands alone as the lowest-ever final-round score by a champion.) Here at St. Andrews, Louis Oosthuizen had begun this Open with a 65, and John Daly, the low American, with a 66. David Hamilton said of Daly that the Scottish galleries really like him, and that Scottish galleries know what they are looking at and are dead silent in the presence of mediocre golf and will have louder applause for strategic high risk—for a certain shot that ends up fifty feet from the flagstick—than for a shot of lower complexity that ends up eighteen inches from the hole. Scottish galleries take to Daly, Hamilton mused, "perhaps because Presbyterians like a sinner."

He mentioned certain "Presbyterian features" of the course—the Valley of Sin, the Pulpit bunker, the bunker named Hell—pointing them out as we passed them. St. Andrews's pot bunkers are nothing like the scalloped sands of other courses. The many dozens of them on the Old Course are small, cylindrical, scarcely wider than a golf swing, and of varying depth—four feet, six feet, but always enough to retain a few strokes. Their faces are vertical, layered, stratigraphic walls of ancestral turf. As you look down a fairway, they suggest the mouths of small caves, or, collectively, the sharp perforations of a kitchen grater. On the sixteenth, he called attention to a pair of them in mid-fairway, only a yard or two apart, with a mound between them that suggested cartilage. The name of this hazard is the Principal's Nose. Hamilton told a joke about a local man playing the course, who suffered a seizure at the Principal's Nose. His playing partner called 999, the U.K. version of 911, and was soon speaking with a person in Bangalore. The playing partner reported the seizure and said that the victim was at the Principal's Nose bunker on the sixteenth hole on the Old Course at St. Andrews, in Scotland; and Bangalore asked, "Which nostril?"

As the Old Course expanded in the nineteenth century from a single track to a closely paralleled double track, seven of the new pairs of fairways ended in common greens, as they do today. These double greens, each sporting two flagsticks, are even weirder than the pot bunkers. Their cardinal feature is immensity. Putts on them are sometimes described in yards rather than feet. An approach shot blown off course can result in a putt with fifty yards to the hole. Standing beside the expanse shared by the fifth and thirteenth flags, David Hamilton said it was the largest. American football teams could play an exhibition game on this green.

While the greens are outsize, the Old Course, as a unit, is much the opposite. Championship golf courses in the United States typically occupy about a hundred and sixty acres. This ancient links course, with its contiguous fairways and longitudinal economy, fits into a hundred and twenty. It is like a printed circuit with its sibling courses on a linksland peninsula between the estuary of the River Eden and the North Sea. When I was twelve years old, I was so naïve that I thought golf links must be called that because the game was played on a sort of chain of consecutive holes. Jimmy Kahny, also in the eighth grade, introduced me to the term as a result of my telling him that I needed money so I could buy an all-weather basketball and dribble my way to school. He said, "There's good money at the golf links, caddying." The good money was one dollar for toting two players' bags, a service known as doubles eighteen. I got my basketball, but—in those caddying seasons—no hint that links were called links before golf was played. The word comes from Old English and refers to a coastal topography behind a beach, a somewhat dunal and undulating landscape, untillable, under bushes of prickly gorse, scattered heather, and a thin turf of marram and other grasses. Scotland is necklaced by these essentially treeless linkslands, brought up from the deep by the crustal rebounding of a region once depressed by glacial ice, links about as vulnerable to sea surges as Los Angeles is to earthquakes, common grazings good for little else but the invention of public games, where marine whirlwinds could blow out the turf and create ancestral bunkers—for example, Turnberry, Muirfield, Dornoch, Crail, Carnoustie, Prestwick, Royal Troon. Carnoustie, to the north of St. Andrews, was just past the Firth of Tay. "If you can't see Carnoustie, it's raining," David Hamilton said. "If you can see Carnoustie, it's going to rain." We could not see Carnoustie. David Hamilton—in moccasins, cotton trousers, a blue shirt, a maroon tie, a beige sweater-vest, and a billed cap that said "The Old Course, St. Andrews Links"—seemed unaware of rain, as befitted the author of *Golf—Scotland's Game* (Partick Press, 1998), an attractively written definitive history, amply and informatively illustrated.

Golf links are wherever you call them that. There's a difference between golf links and links golf. Linksland is where links golf is played. It differs substantially from landlocked, parkland, A to B to C to D golf in this way, among others: it is less linear, and there is greater freedom to select a line from tee to green. For example, on the Old Course players can aim anywhere on the mated fairways. Tiger Woods goes off the first tee to a strategic lie on the eighteenth fairway. Players we watched on the sixteenth were driving up the third to avoid the Principal's Nose. Never mind the occasional high hedgerows of impenetrable gorse, the rippling hay, the patches of heather; most of this wide and treeless panoramic savannah is a carpet of smooth grass; you could all but use a putter from tee to green. It looks easy until you see John Daly hunting for his ball on the third fairway, which, typifying a links fairway, has the loved-in texture of a rumpled sheet. A ball lost in a fairway! A player has five minutes to locate a lost ball, and Daly and his entourage need it. The third fairway, like nearly every other Old Course fairway, has the pit-and-mound topography of a virgin forest, but it wasn't made by trees.

Golf-course architecture has tried to imitate linksland in some most unlikely places (Pennsylvania's Oakmont, on the Appalachian Plateau; California's so-called Pebble Beach Golf Links, on Salinian granite) and to create parkland so universally that countless acres of artificial biosphere have to be sustained on mined water and synthetic chemicals. Rand Jerris remarked that the U.S.G.A. has embarked on a crusade of "sustainability—more sustainable turf grass, use of less water. The ideal of the lush green course is not so ideal anymore. There's a trend toward minimalism in golf-course architecture. Courses by Bill Coore and Ben Crenshaw, for example, move as little dirt as possible." Resonating as this does with the origins of the game itself, golf might do well to get rid of the lush and plush, and go back to the lyrical imprecision of playing over natural country, as the first golfers did on the Old Course, teeing up on wee pyramids of sand and whacking the ball past the sheep toward holes that grew larger by the end of the day. For six hundred years—let alone the Open's hundred and fifty celebrated this summer—golfers on the Old Course have not been able to see where they are going. Links courses generally are described in the sport as blind—all those dunes and mounds hiding greens from tees and fairways. Going out—away from the university town—the golfers and their caddies use an experiential form of dead reckoning. Turning around, they see a skyline of cathedral spires, crenellated battlements, church steeples, and bell towers, and they use them to avoid the invisible bunkers and find the hidden flagsticks on the inward nine.

To one extent or another, an architect can make a simulacrum of all of the above, but what nobody can imitate—you've either got it or you haven't—is wind. Jerris said, "This is not target golf, but more a matter of strategy, choosing your route, so many blind shots. The more you play links golf, the more you understand the subtleties. It takes a lifetime to learn it. Its defense is the wind." Yesterday, a near absence of wind was the main reason so many golfers scored exceptionally low in Round 1 of this 2010 Open. In the eerie calm and after a night of heavy rain, well-aimed shots would stick like darts in cork. Oosthuizen, his saga scarcely begun, was already seven under par—hitting good, loose shots with his technically flawless swing. Among the A.M. threesomes the average score was 71. The average in the afternoon was 73. The difference was a rising but nonetheless substandard wind.

Now, before Round 2 was half over, winds that had been gusting at thirty miles an hour started running thirty in low gear, gusting to forty and fifty. People in the galleries, ignoring rain, were tilting umbrellas ninety degrees to fend off the wind. In grandstands, they wore umbrellas on their backs like capes. The weather made Jerris happy. He called it "true links conditions." Lorne Rubenstein, of the Toronto *Globe and Mail*, the author of *This Round's on Me*, once wrote, "The surprise is that so few players, professionals and amateurs, really get it when it comes to playing links golf." His remark embraced the geometric strategies and all the additional aspects of golf-ball navigation on this trackless green ocean, but it mainly meant coping with the wind. And who might those few players be who really got it? Rubenstein: "Nicklaus, and now Woods, grasp links golf." If the book goes into another printing, he could be adding Oosthuizen, of whom the English golfer Lee Westwood has said, "He flights the ball very well when it gets windy. Has good penetration on his iron shots, and he has obviously got a lot of bottle." "Bottle" is English for unflappable demeanor and nerves of steel. According to Jerris, Tom Watson, who grew up in Kansas City, is "a master" in wind, and golfers from Texas have tended to be wind masters, too—Ben Hogan, Ben Crenshaw, Byron Nelson. "They're good at reading the wind, and at the interaction between wind and topography. A crosswind can put a ball thirty to forty yards off line. Downwind can be even more difficult. Downwind takes spin off the ball. Links golf is more of a ground game than an aerial game like parkland golf. A ball hit lined up with your rear foot has a lower trajectory. The lower they go, the more penetrating the shot is. If they bounce and roll, wind has less effect. If you want to go right or left with the wind, you don't just leave it to the wind; you apply a fade or a draw, too. Hit a draw up into the wind—a shot that bores into the wind. It's like tacking. You can tack in three dimensions—distance, trajectory, direction." Links golf has more than a little in common with regatta sailing. Close hauled. Running before the wind. Jibing over. Luffing. Coming about, hard alee. In irons.

Phil Mickelson, the 2010 Masters champion, understands links golf perhaps better than he plays it. It is just a matter of "taking more club and swinging easier," he said in a pre-Open press interview. He finished tied for forty-eighth. Easy doesn't always do it. Against a stiff wind, you might have to punch hard—a shorter backswing, a shorter follow-through, delofting your club for a lower flight. On the seventh at Pebble Beach, a very short par 3, players have hit 5-irons that would splash in the Pacific if the wind did not blow the ball back. They use, in other words, a hundred-and-ninety-yard club for a hundred-and-ten-yard hole.

Radio Free Fife: "How many pins have the players aimed at this week?"

"Dead aim?"

"Yes."

"None."

Where on earth are these guys?

Jerris: "In a trailer somewhere on the course, monitoring their feeds."

Wind affects putts, too—crosswinds blow them off line, gusts from behind can fatally accelerate a roll downhill. Westwood again: "Everybody thinks when the wind blows it affects the long game most, but it doesn't. It tends to affect the putting the most. The putter is getting blown all over the place, and the ball gets hit by the wind." When the force of the wind reaches forty miles an hour and more, balls that have come to rest on greens may move on their own. The wind putts them. More often the motion is no more than an oscillation. A golfer prepares to putt, and his ball wobbles back and forth as if the earth beneath it were quaking. When balls move on greens, play is suspended, and the several dozen playing players leave the course, to return to their exact positions at some unpredictable time. In this second round of the Open, play was suspended for sixty-five minutes in the early afternoon, but Jerris and I and David Hamilton had already suspended ourselves and were lunching in St. Rule, one of the two women's golf clubs that play on the Old Course.

ST. RULE is on the public street beside the eighteenth green and fairway—on one side, two hundred and fifty yards of contiguous shops, the houses of clubs like St. Rule, and private homes. Unpaying galleries collect on the street to watch golfers finishing their rounds and others, beyond them, hitting off the first tee. This inboard extremity of the Old Course is a world-class cliché in golfing scenes, likely to be on calendars in McMurdo Sound, which makes it no less impressive—the double fairway three hundred and eighty feet wide, the university buildings, and the Royal and Ancient clubhouse like a monopoly token made over time by six architects working in six idioms and finding the offspring of a moated Highland villa and a Florentine castle.

From upstairs bay windows, ladies of St. Rule are watching, too, decorously yielding the view to one another, while members of the St. Andrews Golf Club, all male and in their own bay window a few doors along the fairway, are marginally less yielding. The golf course under these windows belongs to the town and not to any of the golfing clubs, including the Royal and Ancient one. In Scotland, there are relatively few private courses, and few golfing clubs with clubhouses, but every factory, church, hospital, bank, and insurance company has a golf club without a course, and pays green fees at municipal courses. Among the thousands of "club without clubhouse" golfing societies was the one David Hamilton's father—a "minister of religion"—belonged to in Glasgow. Ministers' Monday consisted wholly of clergy who met on Mondays where "they could talk golf and swear." The name of David's wife, Jean Hamilton—a slender, supple athlete with quick dark eyes—was up on a wall of St. Rule as a champion, as were, for example, "Lady Baird-Hay, 1896," and "Lady Anstruther, 1898." Also, Jean belongs to St. Regulus, and she explained the difference: "St. Rule is a ladies' club with a golfing component; St. Regulus members are scratch golfers." Offhandedly, her husband added, "The ladies' clubs are not clamoring for male members."

The University of St. Andrews, brooding above those terminal fairways, is led by a principal whose accession to office has traditionally been accompanied by an automatic membership in the Royal and Ancient Golf Club. In 2009, Louise Richardson became the principal of the University of St. Andrews, the first of her gender, and to date she is not a member of the R&A. David Hamilton kindly showed us through the place, with its varieties of panelled hardwood and its central social Big Room full of deep-leather comfort and—through multipaned windows—a floor-to-ceiling view of the course. In a philosophically Scottish manner, the Big Room doubles as a locker room. Actual panelled-wood lockers line the walls. The place is a form of nude bar, a sanctuary for the nude member. The professional golfers are said to dress in an R&A basement locker room, but they don't. After their rounds, they leave in spikes and go back to their hotels and bed-and-breakfasts. Phil Mickelson leaves in spikes. Louise Richardson does not even arrive in spikes. Born in Ireland, she is a Harvard Ph.D. who was also a Harvard professor before her move to St. Andrews. Her field is political science, and her expertise is in, among other things, terrorism. She plays about as much golf as the Statue of Liberty does. But a tradition is a tradition, an honor can be honorific, and a principle is a principle is a principal.

In real-property terms, the R&A is just an ungainly house on a fragment of an acre between the university and the municipal golf courses, but the R&A is source, arbiter, and guardian of most of the rules of golf, keeper of the political science of golf, and it could use some help. For nearly sixty years, it has shared its world hegemony with the United States Golf Association. No major rule on either side has differed since the R&A gave up the small ball, in 1990. It was about 3.6 per cent smaller than the American ball, and behaved like a bullet in the wind.

Of the three alpha-level all-male clubs in St. Andrews, the two others are the New Golf Club and the St. Andrews Golf Club. Not to put too fine an edge on it, there is class stratigraphy in these organizations. Read up from the St. Andrews Golf Club, which, in a local vulgate, is called the Artisans. Jack Nicklaus is an honorary member. The New Club embraces the middle class. The R&A is a club of "gentlemen." It has two thousand four hundred members, that fine an edge.

We looked in at the Artisans, a four-story hubbub of men holding pints. At the bottom of its atrial stairwell, a sign on the newel post said, "Members are reminded that the Snooker Room is closed until 19 July." David Hamilton said he was a member of the Artisans as well as of the R&A, and he described the Artisans as most populous on Thursdays, because it is the club of shopkeepers, and shopkeepers historically have been busy on Saturdays and off on Thursday afternoons.

I said, incredulously, "You're a shopkeeper?"

He said, "I have a printing shop."

Off we went for coffee and to see his printing shop at his house on North Street in the middle of town. In a stone shed between house and garden were two hot-metal presses, gleaming with mechanical health in a cluttered space more suitable for potting. In racks overhead were upwards of fifty hickory-shafted golf clubs. This was Partick Press, where he prints what he calls his "short, arcane things." For example? "A poem on student golf." When Partick published *Golf—Scotland's Game*, in 1998, it was printed in Edinburgh. "All the various studies were headed toward a big book," he said. "I wanted complete control, so I published it myself."

Most people in David Hamilton's profession prefer complete control. He was teaching medicine at Oxford in the nineteen-eighties when he followed an avocational interest and "took instruction in letterpress." He and Jean had little money, and to finance this two-year "sabbatical" from his work in Glasgow they went for a fortnight every couple of months to Baghdad, where he performed kidney transplants for Iraqis. In the United Kingdom, he was an early practitioner of organ-transplant surgery, the author of classic papers in medical journals. He has written a book called *A History of Organ Transplantation* (2012). His other books include *The Healers: A History of Medicine in Scotland* (1981) and *The Monkey Gland Affair* (1986), which cast something heavier than heavy doubt on the claims of a Russian surgeon to have restored erectile function in humans by implanting tissue from the testicles of monkeys.

Remarking on his years in Oxford, he said, "It was a midlife escapade. They regarded me as an amiable eccentric." He was a six-handicap golfer, and back in Glasgow he became an occasional champion of the Western Infirmary Golf Club. Retired from surgery since 2004, he teaches each year about a hundred and fifty future doctors as a lecturer in medicine at the University of St. Andrews.

I asked, "Are they all undergraduates?"

"We say 'students' in Scotland," he replied. "They say 'undergraduates' in England."

On the way to his house, we had passed a university door on which block lettering said in gold: "STUDENT EXPERIENCE OFFICE."

We had dinner at the New Golf Club with David and Jean Hamilton as guests of their friends and neighbors David and Ruth Malcolm. A St. Andrews native with auld Scotland in his ruddy face and pure Fife in his lilting voice, David Malcolm is the co-author (with Peter E. Crabtree) of *Tom Morris of St. Andrews: The Colossus of Golf 1821–1908* (2008). The book is not only a biography of the caddie-player-greenkeeper-clubmaker who was the sport's most famous figure in the nineteenth century but also, as wider history, the peer of David Hamilton's *Golf—Scotland's Game*. There is a society in St. Andrews called the Literati of the Links whose members meet now and again to talk golf history and discuss one another's monographs. The two Davids are Literati. At Prestwick, in Ayrshire, Tom Morris won four Opens. Tiger Woods has won three. Tom Morris became Old Tom Morris after his son Tom Morris won four more. In a hundred and fifty years, twenty-two Scottish golfers have won the Open—three since the First World War. This nostalgic macaroon is more than enough to set David Hamilton onto what he calls "the golfing diaspora" of Scottish professional golfers, immigrating a century ago to the United States and Canada. In his words, "It was a black hole in professional golf in Britain. The sudden decline in Open champions was because young men were leaving Scotland in huge numbers. In Scotland, they were working class, treated as inferiors. Working-class kids from Carnoustie and St. Andrews would be immediately pigeonholed in England, but not in North America. In America, they may have been gruff and taciturn, but they were classy." The Morrises remained autochthonous. In 1902, Old Tom Morris helped found the New Golf Club, on the third floor of which we were dining by windows overlooking the Old Course. In 1908, Old Tom fell down the New Club stairway and did not survive.

Play had resumed, but the wind had not much subsided. If the MetLife blimp were to take off here and now, it would soon be in Yorkshire. Blimps and Scotland are contradictions in terms. The BBC looks down on the golfers from Guinness-record cherry pickers. Even our own altitude, in the New Golf Club dining room, was enough to make particularly evident the contrast between the two sides of the planet's widest fairway. Below us, the eighteenth-hole side was wrinkled with mounds and deep hollows, including the Valley of Sin—the depressed apron of the eighteenth green, something like a large deep bunker full of sod. The eighteenth side, like nearly all of the Old Course, was an image of its former self—ancestral linksland topography. Beyond the eighteenth and down the eastern side— below the first tee—was a sweep of ground unnaturally smooth. David Malcolm explained that it was "reclaimed" land. Hulls of old herring boats, loaded up with rock, had been positioned there to anchor new ground filled in around them. The project had also roofed a sewer, he said, that ran out from the town. When the sewer flooded, armies of large rats ran into the R&A.

After dinner, in the all but endless summer daylight, Jerris and I return to the course, and to the wind-chilled grandstand over the seventeenth tee, one of three fixed positions from which we have decided to watch things from day to day unfold, another being above the seventeenth green. In the defenseless calm of the first round, as various players have remarked, all but one hole was easy; the seventeenth was, as ever, "impossible." A dogleg par 4 newly stretched to four hundred and ninety-five yards, it presents an arresting scenario. The tee shot is completely blind and eliminates the bend by going over a large, elongate shed. The golfers confront its north-facing wall and aim across a sign above which nothing is visible but sky. The sign says:

OLD COURSE HOTEL
St. Andrews
Golf Resort & Spa

The shed is a part of the grand hotel, and close on the right are a great many guest-room windows. To the left of the sign is a lion rampant. A pusillanimous shot is a drive hit over the lion rampant. Wind heavily influences the selection of vector, but, generally speaking, a reasonable choice is over the "O" in OLD, and there is high risk and big money in the "O" in HOTEL.

The fairway is scarcely fifteen yards wide at its narrowest. In Jerris's words, "You are hitting over out of bounds to a fairway you can't see. The fairway is a right-hand dogleg fade, but if you fade it too much"—as you influence the ball to curl to the right—"you are back on the tee hitting 3." Psychologically unbalanced by this possibility, golfers "get quick," roll their hands as they swing, close the club face, and send the ball into too big a draw to the left and into hay that is less suitable for rough than for harvest. Brute strength is needed to get out and reach the green. After Angel Cabrera hits his second shot to some other destination, hay is hanging from his follow-through like Spanish moss. The longest successful drive we see on seventeen is by the American sinner John Daly, wearing slacks meant to resemble the skin of a red-and-black tiger. Daly won the Open at St. Andrews in 1995, ballooned in weight in subsequent years, did some rehab, and now has an implanted turnbuckle around the upper end of his stomach, like a great cormorant on the Yangtze River.

Because an asphalt thoroughfare runs beside the green and some of the fairway, the seventeenth is known as the Road Hole. Small and narrow and shaped like a kidney, the green is one of the four on the Old Course that have only one flagstick. The celebrated Road Hole bunker—straight-walled, cylindrical, five feet deep—fits so snugly into the kidney's indentation that it can virtually be regarded as a bunker in the middle of a green. From the grandstand above the green, the wider view right to left a hundred and eighty degrees is of the crowds on the public street, the eighteenth green, the university, the R&A clubhouse, the media's big white tent, the North Sea rolling toward the beach where the British runners ran in the film classic *Chariots of Fire*, the coast across the water on its way to Dundee, and the shed that makes this hole the blindest on the course. Players on the tee are as invisible to us as we are to them, so we don't see them hitting. Balls just appear on the fairway, seemingly out of nowhere, or they disappear elsewhere, while we stare at the old shed in anticipation of the players who will come around it next, like scouts coming over a ridge.

A yellow golf ball appears. I ask Jerris whose it might be.

"Hirofumi Miyase's," he says.

"And how do you know that?"

"Because he's playing with Steven Tiley, and there's no way an Englishman is going to use a yellow ball."

This is the third round now, and the flag is out straight in the stiff wind. Henrik Stenson, seven under coming into seventeen and tied for the best score of the day, gets into the Road Hole bunker, is compelled by his lie to come out in an ersatz direction, and is no longer tied for the best score of the day. The pin is positioned close to the road, with short steep rough and a cinder path between, and a few feet behind the road is a stone wall that would not look amiss in New England. Watching bogey after double bogey, we see errant balls bump-and-running beside the green and going up against the wall, or bouncing on the asphalt and over the wall. "The wall on seventeen is an immovable obstruction from which you don't get relief," Jerris says. "It is not a T.I.O.—a temporary immovable obstruction, like a TV tower or a grandstand. At this stone wall, there's no relief."

Comes Mickelson and he is over the road and close to the wall with room barely for a short swing. He smacks a great shot against the short, steep greenside rough; the ball pops up, continues, and comes to rest near the hole. In Southern California, behind the house he grew up in, Mickelson's parents installed a golf green with a short-game practice area in the way that other people install swimming pools. But he misses this putt and is down in bogey five. Miguel Ángel Jiménez will soon appear, and go so close to the wall that he has no open swing whatever, so he punches the shot straight into the stone wall, and it ends up behind him on the green.

Most of the entourages walking with the golfers and caddies number about twelve—marshals, scorer, standard bearer, R&A rules official, forward observer, and so forth. Woods and Darren Clarke come around the shed with an entourage two and a half times the usual size, starting with extra marshals. Clarke is out of bounds by the hotel. Woods is in the hay. He blasts out, goes into more hay. His third shot ignores the green. It crosses the cinder path, crosses the asphalt road, and stops a club length from the stone wall. Woods conjures a high parabola that sits down close to the hole. Jerris calls it "the ultimate cut shot, a parachute shot." It saves a bogey, but not a major.

Comes Rory McIlroy around the shed, and his second shot is so close to the stone wall that he can only hit his next one away from the green. In the wild winds of the second round, the Old Course rebuked him with an 80. Now he takes a double bogey—on his way, however, to a 69.

A time comes when the groups that like clockwork appear around the shed have stopped appearing like clockwork around the shed. The spectators in the grandstand by the green stare at the shed as if to make things happen, but nothing happens; the shed seems to have more past than future. As if the seventeenth, across time, had not developed within and around itself enough unusual hazards, a railroad ran up it until fifty years ago and was not out of bounds. The shed had been built for storing coal and curing golf-club hickory, which the trains dropped off. Only golfers are overdue now.

Vijay Singh appears around the shed. The Big Fijian is deliberate. Read: slow. He takes his time, and yours. He has also taken home as much as ten million dollars in a year. He is a Masters champion and a P.G.A. champion (twice), and has won the FedEx Cup—a résumé that has not made him overly selective about where he plays. He is as professional as it is possible to be, signing on for more tournaments worldwide than almost anyone. Golf pays well, and Singh may take his time but he is on hand to be paid. Even with his easygoing liquid swing, he bogeys the hole.

From this same grandstand perch, the eighteenth tee and the great home fairway are right in front of us as well, where the Swilken Burn, straight-sided and in cross section no less engineered than the Los Angeles River, leaves town in ampersand fashion on its leisurely way, across the eighteenth and the first, to the sea. Player after player, released from the seventeenth, explodes up the final fairway—par 4, three hundred and fifty yards— and lots of them drive the green. Birdies gather. And while the guys on eighteen go up the killing ground, Louis Oosthuizen and Mark Calcavecchia, playing in our direction, hit off from the first tee, each about to bogey. They are the last twosome—No. 1 and No. 2 halfway through the championship—but Calcavecchia will disintegrate today, taking nine strokes on the fifth and finishing in 77. Not so Oosthuizen, who is expected to crack but will not. Seeming less tense than a length of string, he walks down the first, his caddie beside him.

Oosthuizen's caddie is a black South African nearly twice his age—one of few black caddies on the European tour. His name is Zack Rasego. He lives in Soweto, has worked for Oosthuizen for seven years, and was once Gary Player's caddie. Frustrated by missing so many cuts in recent weeks, Oosthuizen decided that he needed a fresh caddie, and so he told Zack Rasego that after the Open the two of them would be parting ways.

AT THE ANCIENT TRACK'S REMOTE END—where the Old Course makes the turn—are five tees, five flagsticks, and three greens, collectively known as the Loop:

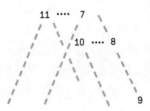

It is a sequence of holes so hallowed in the game that Amen Corner, at Augusta National, has been compared with it, but while the Loop is far more complex geometrically, as golf goes it is less difficult. Birdies are to be made, just lying there for the taking, unless the wind is blowing hard, which it nearly always is. This prow of the linksland is much like the bow of a ship in the winter North Atlantic.

In the experience of David Fay, the executive director of the United States Golf Association, the grandstand above the 10-8 green in the Loop, which also looks over the crisscrossing fairways that lead to 11-7, has "the best view in all of sports." He may not have consulted with Spike Lee. He may have avoided Jack Nicholson. Nonetheless, the place is breathless in every meaning of the word, as the cold wind bends the simplest of shots and penetrates every layer of every fabric armed against it. If you are in the top row and the wind is coming over your back, seagulls hang motionless and stare into your eyes, a club length from your face. It's a Brueghelian scene against the North Sea, with golfers everywhere across the canvas—putting here, driving there, chipping and blasting in syncopation, but being too smart to loft a wedge lest the ball be blown to the streets of St. Andrews a mile and a half away. When we turn around, the rest of the course is visible, all the way back to the masonry of the medieval town: golfers and galleries stopping and moving, moving and stopping—it's like watching a Swiss astronomical clock reacting to the arrival of noon. The dark marching lines of the galleries cross fairways in hooded parkas, in rain pants—serious, this. They are much grayer, these Scottish cognoscenti, than, say, a gallery in California. They are mainly from Edinburgh and Glasgow, in addition to the locals from Fife, and they appear to be of an age with the parents and grandparents of American galleries.

As course design, the X point in the Loop, where the eleventh and seventh fairways cross, may have been thought out by the same ram and ewe that caused West Fourth Street to wander all over Greenwich Village and eventually intersect West Twelfth. Jerris remarks that when Bobby Jones played through the Loop in his first Open, in 1921, he hit across the X, went into a bunker, came out ripping up his scorecard, and walked off the course. In 1958, he was made a freeman of the Town of St. Andrews—the first American so honored since Benjamin Franklin.

Morning on the Loop, Round 4, and a chill wind is blowing.

On-course radio: "There really isn't any wind to think about now."

Jerris: "Not in their trailer."

Vijay Singh makes the turn, strolling around the Loop. Think sixty minutes to go through a revolving door.

Ryo Ishikawa, three under par, hits to fifteen feet on the tenth, and holes the putt. He is eighteen years old. A few months ago, in a tournament on the Japan Golf Tour, he shot a 58. From St. Andrews, tied for twenty-seventh, he will take home four million yen. For thirteen years, the bright aura of Tiger Woods put the field behind him into relative twilight. Woods was like a screen saver, or some sort of curtain or scrim, veiling what else might be seen. Now and again, directors clicked on Phil Mickelson and others, but the focus of narrative attention was Tiger Woods, cameras buzzing his every stroke like horseflies. Now that the scrim has been removed, not the least of the dividends is the montage of young and outstanding golfers—like Ishikawa, like Oosthuizen—going by. The German Martin Kaymer, twenty-five, will gross $186,239 in a tie for seventh, as will the Americans Sean O'Hair, twenty-eight, and Nick Watney, twenty-nine. Rory McIlroy will tie for third despite his 80 in the second round, and he will collect $394,237. Before the 80, McIlroy had played nine rounds of tournament golf on the Old Course at St. Andrews, among which his worst score was 69. In May, at Quail Hollow, in Charlotte, he shot a final-round 62 to win $1,170,000 and beat Phil Mickelson by four strokes. Five years ago at Royal Portrush in Northern Ireland, where the Open was once played, McIlroy shot a 61 and set the course record. He was sixteen years old. And Rickie Fowler, aged twenty-one, comes into the Loop dressed in hunter orange, blaze "orange from head to toe—shoes, pants, belt, shirt, hat, bracelet, necklace, it's my school colors, I went to Oklahoma State!" Radio Free Fife says he "looks like a prisoner." So far this year, Fowler's first full year on the tour, he has twice finished second and has won more than two million dollars. He will add $87,839 today, as he ties for fourteenth, like South Carolina's Dustin Johnson, aged twenty-six, and the

Korean Jin Jeong, twenty; but Jeong will get nothing—he's an amateur.

Out in the Open are old guys, too. Here John Daly comes into the Loop with an entourage of twenty-one people. Daly's habiliments change daily. He now has stars on his right leg and stripes down his left leg—red, white, and blue. Red jacket. White cap. When Ian Poulter, of Buckinghamshire, appeared in clothes derived from the Union Jack, it was said that he looked as if he were about to be buried at sea. Jerris says Daly is dressed for a Princeton reunion, but I would put him in any town's parade on the Fourth of July. He shot a 66 in the first round. He is now one over for the Open. On the seventh, he hits an iron off the tee to lay up short of a bunker, then a dare-the-wind wedge to twenty feet past the hole, then a lagged putt and in for a par. The grandstand is wild for him. "He plays fast," Jerris says. "Scots like that. They play faster than we do." After Daly drives off the eleventh tee and nears the end of the Loop, there's a mass exodus from the grandstand.

IN THE AFTERNOON, Jerris and I split up—he to stay on the course, I to go into the Media Centre. After Tiger Woods scored 67 in the first round and went to the Media Centre for a press interview, the crush of spectators outside the tent was so heavy that hundreds were gridlocked on foot, compressed, unable to move. A Scottish voice in the crunch asked, "And what did he end up shooting?" To which a Scottish voice replied: "His missus." To the extent that there is any crush outside the tent now, it is caused by the media crowding in to watch the climactic holes of the 2010 Open on the BBC feed.

The Media Centre is sixty yards long and thirty yards wide, or enough to provide desk space, Internet access, and free food to five hundred journalists—not to mention swiftly distributed transcriptions of all player interviews, the common source for essentially every line of dialogue that goes out into the print world. The atmosphere is less bookish than bookie-ish. Along one side is a full-field scoreboard that resembles a tote board in an off-track betting parlor. It is not electronic, though. Its many numbers are changed by hand by women on sliding ladders. At either end is the BBC—golfers in action on silent screens about the size of sheets of plywood. Heavy rain on the tent roof can be so loud that nobody would hear the audio anyway. It helps to have an on-course radio around your neck. My assigned space is between Peter Stone, of *The Sydney Morning Herald*, and Brian Viner, of *The Independent*. In our immediate surroundings are *The Detroit News*, the *Tokyo Shimbun*, *The Augusta Chronicle*, *The Charlotte Observer*, the Golf Press Association, *Desert Golf Magazine*, and a line of laptops from the Associated Press. As the Open nears its end, more people are in here than have been in here at any other time all week. When those British runners in *Chariots of Fire* came off the beach and jumped a fence and headed toward the first tee, they ran right through the Media Centre, in a manner of speaking.

Stewart Cink, the defending champion, finishes the eighteenth one over par. Tied for forty-eighth, he will barely make it home to Georgia with $21,130. After a three-hundred-and-fifty-six-yard drive that stops two feet from the flagstick, Tom Lehman eagles the eighteenth ($87,839). Meanwhile, the on-course radio is impressed enough with Louis Oosthuizen to jinx him into the Valley of Sin, the Principal's Nose, and the Swilken Burn. He is "totally relaxed," "looks unstoppable," "looks very solid indeed," and has it "just the way he wants it to be—a one-horse race."

Gradually, as I listen to the radio and watch the tote board and the television images, dawn cracks and I come to realize that the BBC is the only feed that the on-course radio commentators have. They are not out there, as imagined, rolling around in some mobile home with windscreen wipers and video-cam monitors. Like all the other journalists in five or six media, they are doing their reporting from inside this tent.

Paul Casey, who is English and almost thirty-three, is with Oosthuizen in the final pairing, having begun the day eleven under and four strokes behind. If the Open championship is to result in any kind of duel, most likely it will happen here. But while they match each other hole for hole, they walk along chattering, joking, laughing, failing to act as if a drive here or a chip there could be worth more than a few hundred thousand pounds. My pendant radio says to me, "It's all going to start to happen down in the Loop."

Down in the Loop, Oosthuizen bogeys the eighth while Casey makes par. Grandstand and gallery, the crowd waxes partisan with a Great British roar. It seems loud enough to crack concrete, but perhaps not loud enough to crack Oosthuizen. Casey, with the honor, now drives the ninth green—three hundred and fifty-seven yards—again detonating the crowd. Oosthuizen looks down steadily at his glove, now tees up, drives, and also reaches the green, but closer to the flagstick and on a better line. Casey putts for eagle. Misses. Oosthuizen putts for eagle and the ball rolls in. There is a red spot on Oosthuizen's glove. He put it there to help him concentrate. He continually glances at it as if it were a coach.

Again chattering and joking, Oosthuizen and Casey come to the twelfth hole, where Oosthuizen's drive carries five mid-fairway bunkers and rolls out between islands of gorse, leaving only a short pitch to the green. There is an aggregate acre of gorse. Casey goes into it. R&A marshals plunge into the bushes, searching—a brave thing to do among the concertina spines. Playing yesterday with Oosthuizen, Mark Calcavecchia also went into gorse. He played a provisional ball, but after he was told that his ball had been found he picked up the provisional and went to play the found ball. It wasn't his. Penalized stroke-and-distance for the lost ball and another stroke for lifting the provisional ball, he ended up with a 9, and it was ciao, Calcavecchia. Now, standing idle in the cold wind during the search for Casey's ball, Oosthuizen pulls on a sweater. If nothing else can affect his momentum, maybe it can be frozen. After Casey's ball is found unplayable, Casey takes a drop, with a stroke penalty. Radio Free Fife says, "It smells like a 7." Whatever the smell of a 7 might be, Casey very quickly is in a position to describe it. His shot flies over the green. Oosthuizen birdies with a fifteen-foot putt, and the duel is over; but before he can bury the corpse Oosthuizen still has to drag it twenty-four hundred yards. Walking up the eighteenth fairway, his final drive just off the green, and seven strokes ahead of the entire field, Oosthuizen at last permits himself (as he soon tells a tentful of reporters) to think that he has won his first major, and to say to himself reassuringly, "I'm definitely not going to ten-putt." He also reports that, walking up there, he thought of Nelson Mandela. This morning before coming to the golf course, Oosthuizen learned on the Internet that this is Mandela's ninety-second birthday.

Michael Brown, the chairman of the R&A's championship committee, thanks the Town of St. Andrews for the use of the golf course. Oosthuizen receives the Claret Jug, his name engraved upon it. Waiting for the press to finish assembling in the Media Centre, he sits on a stage, holds the trophy like a book, and reads it.

Medium: "When did you know you weren't going to choke?"

Oosthuizen, grinning: "That's pretty mean, saying 'choke.'"

Medium: "It seemed remarkable that you and Paul were chatting away when there was such a big prize at stake."

Oosthuizen: "We have a lot of fun on the course. It's still just a game you're playing. Otherwise, it's going to be quite miserable."

Between them, Oosthuizen and Casey have just received more than a million pounds. It was the only game in town.

At eight under par, Casey has tied for third with Henrik Stenson and Rory McIlroy. At nine under, Lee Westwood is second (half a million pounds). At sixteen under, Oosthuizen becomes one of the few golfers in history to win a major by seven or more strokes, a list that includes Nicklaus and Woods. A list of those who did not includes Ben Hogan, Byron Nelson, Sam Snead, and Bobby Jones.

Medium: "You had a temper at one time. It boggles many of us to see how calm you are. Did you get any help to get over that?"

Oosthuizen: "It's just a matter of growing up, really."

Oosthuizen's caddie, Zack Rasego, interviewed by on-course radio: "What's it like to caddy for him?"

Rasego: "It's a mixed bag, to be honest with you."

Radio: "What is your drink of choice?"

Rasego: "Whisky."

Radio (aside): "He's in the right place."

He is also secure in his job, Oosthuizen heaping praise and gratitude on him for many things, from his reading of putts to his bolstering advice down the stretch ("You've hit your driver so well—just hit it"). Rasego's share of the prize is eighty-five thousand pounds.

Rasego: "It's good to win for South Africa on Nelson Mandela's birthday today. It's a fantastic day for us."

Oosthuizen: "What he's done for our country is unbelievable. So happy birthday to him once again."

This is the extent to which Oosthuizen was troubled by St. Andrews's remorseless wind: "The thing is that wind, to me, it's a nice wind to use a little cut up against." Growing up in the Cape winds, Oosthuizen, son of a struggling farmer, was trained and educated at the expense of a foundation set up by Ernie Els, who did not make the cut in this 2010 Open. In Open history, Oosthuizen is the fourth Open champion from South Africa. Ernie Els was the third. Before him, Gary Player won it three times. To encourage Oosthuizen and to offer him advice, Gary Player called him this morning, and spoke with him in Afrikaans.

The first Open champion from South Africa was Arthur D'Arcy (Bobby) Locke in his plus-fours and with his hickory-shafted gooseneck putter winning the Open four times.

Medium: "Do you know much about Bobby Locke?"

Oosthuizen, with jug: "Unfortunately, I don't. Yeah, unfortunately, I don't."

In 2009, Bill Tierney resigned as the men's lacrosse coach at Princeton and became the men's lacrosse coach at the University of Denver. He had won six national championships at Princeton, and now he was making, in every respect, including geography, a spectacular jump downscale. I had come to know him well and needless to say regretted his departure, but my interest in the game particularly had to do with its growth—its spreading out from Eastern enclaves—and this was the best example yet.

How would Bill do? Out there in Colorado, how would he get things going? This is how he got things going.

Pioneer

IN COATS AND TIES, THE UNIVERSITY OF DENVER MEN'S
lacrosse team caught the five o'clock tumbrel to the Carrier
Dome. It was actually a chartered bus, and the ride from their
hotel was scarcely a mile, but this characteristically boisterous
group was silent now, on its way to face off with Syracuse, the
No. 1 team in the college world, national champions in 2008,
national champions in 2009.

At the Carrier Dome, you could begin to sense hostility
even before you stepped inside. The Carrier Dome is a large, in-
flated tent—capacity forty-nine thousand—and, if certain doors

are not opened and shut in correct sequence, air can come blasting out at Force 11. If you make it to and past the first door, a second one might suddenly swing shut so hard it could crush a hand, and has done so. Negotiating the air locks, the Denver team was victorious in reaching its locker room. Denver was undefeated. Syracuse was undefeated. For both teams, this was the first game of the 2010 season.

Five months earlier, the Denver coach noticed that Syracuse had nothing on its schedule for February 19th, the first day anybody in Division I of the N.C.A.A. was allowed to schedule a lacrosse game. He telephoned John Desko, the Syracuse coach, and asked him if he would like to open his season against Denver. No problem about the travel, he assured Desko; Denver would be pleased to come east. In the old Western world of the quarter horse—of itinerant peddlers and country tracks—this was known as "jumping a trader for a race." The two coaches knew each other well. Three times, they had been the final two. Desko at Syracuse had won five national championships. Bill Tierney, the Denver coach, had won six national championships as head coach at Princeton. Over all, they are, as record books render it, the two "winningest active coaches" in the game.

In June, just after the 2009 season, in his ivied-tower office high above a Princeton gym, Tierney got a call from Denver, asking for advice on the selection of a new lacrosse coach, the job being vacant. In mid-conversation, Denver said, out of nowhere, "What would it take to bring you here?" Tierney stopped the shot and looked for the outlet pass. Of the sixty Division I men's lacrosse teams, only Denver and the Air Force Academy were west of the Mississippi. A few decades ago, U.S. lacrosse players of all ages were numbered in the hundreds and played for East Coast schools. Now, male and female, there are five hundred thousand U.S. lacrosse players, and their schools are in Texas, California, Oregon, Washington, and many other Western states. The explosion is so current that some six hundred high-school lacrosse teams are coming into being every year. Nowhere is the Western expansion greater than in Colorado, where lacrosse goals line the mountain front from Cañon City to Fort Collins, where the Vail Lacrosse Shootout draws two thousand participants, and where the one-day LaxFest at Dick's Sporting Goods Park, in Commerce City, involves more than two hundred teams and five thousand players.

Tierney, who grew up in Levittown, on Long Island, and played at Cortland State and was an assistant at Johns Hopkins before his years at Princeton, could go to Denver, improve its already accomplished team, serve a deep commitment to the geographical reach of the game, earn more money, offer athletic scholarships, and hire his older son, Trevor, already a resident of Denver, as his assistant coach. That was what it took to take him there.

The Eastern lacrosse world reacted to the news as if a Vince Lombardi had left the N.F.L. to teach American football at Harrow. All publications that cover lacrosse, and even some that seldom do, were full of puzzlement and surprise, and the most employed word was "shock." How could he leave Princeton? It can be done. And Tierney knew what he was doing. He was going to live through the hype (as he described his early summer), get out to Denver, and start teaching. When he picked up that phone and called John Desko, he was not just jumping the national champion to give his boys experience. He actually meant to go east and beat Syracuse. "I felt I needed to justify myself to the team," he said in Syracuse on the eve of the game.

"There had been so much hype about my coming there. I wasn't bringing lacrosse to Denver. This team was well established in Division I and was one of the sixteen in the tournament last year." Arriving at the Carrier Dome, he said, "All right, guys. This is what we've been waiting for."

They had been there practicing the day before, and the coach was impressed to notice how unintimidated they seemed. They did not gawk. They were not struck dumb by the three-tiered palace with private suites, by the championship banners, by the eight-hundred-square-foot hanging tapestry of Jimmy Brown, featuring side-by-side pictures of Brown in his football uniform and Brown holding his lacrosse stick high for a right-handed shot, the words "Greatest Player Ever" running under and connecting the two pictures. Jimmy Brown was not going to play tomorrow.

Tierney called a huddle to review the actual opposition, mentioning a rare danger in three defensive midfielders all hungry to break out and score, mentioning a Syracuse player "who wants to shoot every time he gets the ball," mentioning the unusual number of Syracuse players who favor the left side, and another who is a "great finisher. More dodge and shoot than a passer. We can slide to him." He mentioned Chris Daniello ("left-hander, tries to go to goal really hard"), John Lade ("best defenseman"), Joel White, Jovan Miller, Stephen Keogh, and, especially, "big, powerful, left-handed" Cody Jamieson.

"But this is not about them," he said. "It is about how we play defense. When we have the ball, dodge hard, throw simple passes, take simple shots—don't try anything fancy." One of his players would try a behind-the-back shot in the game. Three of his starters were from Colorado, one each from Ontario, Connecticut, Maine, Minnesota, and California, and two from Texas (small identical athletic twins, both in the midfield). On Denver's over-all roster, twenty-five per cent were from Colorado and more from the East, but none from Baltimore or Long Island, primal hotbeds of U.S. lacrosse. When Tierney began his second year at Princeton, in the fall of 1988, he outlined to his astonished freshmen—the first group he had recruited—what they would have to do to win a national championship. Eyes rolled. Glances oscillated. Somebody may have twirled a finger beside an ear. A national what? Tierney's 1988 team had won two, lost thirteen. Princeton had lost forty-six games in four years, and had not won an Ivy League championship in twenty-one. The N.C.A.A. tournament was as far off its scale as the Bowl Championship Series is to Princeton football teams. Yet those freshmen with the rolling eyes went to Philadelphia four years later and beat Syracuse in the national final in double overtime. Now, at the practice in the Dome, Tierney ended his remarks to his Denver players by mentioning "the importance of presenting an air of confidence at the opening whistle."

NEXT EVENING in the locker room and dressed for the game, Denver was not presenting an air of confidence. They had brought techno with them and were being jackhammered by two loudspeakers. Two players had squatted low and were doing face-offs on the carpet, while the majority sat on folding chairs in front of their lockers and stared straight ahead. When the techno went silent, it revealed their silence. A percentage, not a small one, collected in a corner, knelt together, and prayed. When all had returned to their chairs, Trevor Tierney, the first assistant coach, led them through their psychological preparation.

"Sit up as you would on your blocks in yoga," he said. With

their hands tightly clasped and their eyes closed, they were like passengers on a jet in heavy turbulence. There were long pauses between phases of the preparation. The second phase was Third-Person Visualization. This was not the same planet that Trevor's father had played on, but he sat as quietly as his team while Trevor spun out the hypnotics of modern sports psychology. Visualization is what golfers do. You imagine the ball where you want to hit it, imagine every aspect of its flight thereto. In this milieu, Trevor told them to watch themselves in action. "Picture yourself as if you're watching a highlight reel of yourself making big plays throughout the game, making big hits, picking up ground balls—as if you are watching yourself do it," he said, and then paused for a couple of minutes while they watched themselves on their internal TVs.

When Trevor spoke again, he said, "If you are feeling nervous, nervous is good. All right? It makes us stop thinking about things. It makes us ready to play. If you're nervous, that's fine. Feel nervous." This Trevor, who is thirty-one, is a film-star-handsome dark-haired dude, who wore to the Carrier Dome a silver tie and a dark blue pinstriped three-piece suit. He was now in his Denver assistant's sweats. In the 1998 N.C.A.A. quarter-final, Duke jumped out to a devastating lead over Princeton, and the Princeton season appeared to be over. What to do? Head Coach Tierney pulled his starting goalie and sent his freshman son, Trevor, into the net. If Duke had continued to widen its lead and the game had ended in a blowout, a tragedian might have seen possibilities in the story. It was something like the Alcázar de Toledo in the Spanish Civil War when the Falangist colonel was under siege in the palace and was called on the telephone by the attacking Republicans, saying, Colonel, we have your son—surrender in ten minutes or he dies.

According to the story as perpetuated by the Falangists, the colonel asked to speak to his son. After the Republicans put the boy on the phone, the colonel said to him, "Commend your soul to God, shout '*Viva España*,' and die like a hero." Making stop after amazing stop, Trevor stuffed Duke and stuffed them some more, while the Princeton attack passed Duke going away. Trevor was twice All-American, and in his last college game—another N.C.A.A. final—his team beat Syracuse 10–9 in overtime.

Now he was saying to the Denver team, "If you're scared, there's nothing to be scared about. If you're scared, you're thinking about what's going to happen: 'What am I going to do wrong? How can I fail?' You're not going to fail. Picture all those Syracuse guys. They're ranked No. 1. They're all spread out. We are all together. If we play hard tonight, there is no one and no team that can stop us."

Bill Tierney had the last word before his Denver Pioneers took the field. He told his players what it had been like for him coming to the Carrier Dome in earlier years. As he appeared on the field behind his team, heavy words always came down upon him: "Fuck you, coach! You suck! Your team is going to get blown out!" This time, he said, people he had already encountered in the Dome were saying things like "Good luck, coach" and "Hope it goes well, coach," in tones a kindly warden might use to someone eating his last meal. "This game is about dodging hard, getting out of each other's way, and shooting the daylights out of the ball," Tierney said. He spoke of "the importance of clears"—they could make "a five- or six-goal swing in a game like this." And he said, "Just get up the field and push the thing down their throat. Any questions on that? Since June, fellas, this whole thing has sometimes been about me. It's about us now. It's us. It's we. This journey is going to be about 'us' and 'we.' I'm tired of 'me.' What I want it to be is 'you.' This crowd, they're real nice now, but we're going to come out there tonight and we're going to play our asses off, with our hearts, with our legs, and with our heads. And the next time we come, I want to hear 'Fuck you, coach.' All right, let's go get 'em." The Pioneers erupted in a roar, and ran out onto the field.

NINETY-THREE SECONDS into the action, Alex Demopoulos scored for Denver. Trevor Tierney was pacing the sideline as much as his father was. If their relationship in Trevor's undergraduate years was Shakespearian, so was this. At 8:39 of the first quarter, John Dickenson, one of the identical twins, out of Highland Park High School, in Dallas, scored for Denver. Early in the second quarter, Bill Tierney was screaming at a referee, "Hey, Mike! Up in the face! They can't do that." Trevor put an arm on his father. Evidently the team's shrink, Trevor was equally mindful of the head coach, ready to do what he could to calm him when necessary, which is not a part-time job. At Princeton, Bryce Chase, a volunteer assistant coach who was also a trial lawyer, hovered close to Tierney during every game, to muffle what he could muffle, and help avoid technicals. A year or two ago, Tierney, shouting, laid a string of slanderous words on a passing referee, and that very referee was one of the three officials before him now, working this game in the Carrier Dome. (Tierney: "It's not a problem. He's used to it.") At 2:53 of the second quarter, Todd Baxter, out of Eden Prairie High School, in Minnesota, scored for Denver. Four minutes into the third, Denver's Alex Demopoulos scored again (Avon Old Farms School, Connecticut). He would score twice more. And

Andrew Lay (Denver East High School) would intercept a Syracuse pass and drill a goal from thirty feet. Unfortunately (for Denver), this montage of Denver goals was insufficient.

So let's roll back the clock and start again: Forty-one seconds after the opening face-off, Jovan Miller (Christian Brothers Academy, Syracuse, New York) scored for Syracuse. Twelve seconds later, Kevin Drew (John Jay High School, Cross River, New York) scored for Syracuse. The game was not yet one minute old. A minute and a half later, Max Bartig (Northport High School, Northport, New York) scored for Syracuse. Jeremy Thompson, out of Lafayette High School, in Lafayette, New York, was doing the face-offs for Syracuse, with his braided pigtail hanging Iroquois-style down his back all the way across his number to his waist. And why not? He's an Onondaga. This was north-central New York, where the Iroquois developed this form of this game, and where they have lived for seven thousand years. Onondaga, Cayuga, Mohawk—on Syracuse's 2010 men's and women's lacrosse teams, three of the Six Nations of the Iroquois are represented by one or more athletes.

Big, powerful, left-handed Cody Jamieson scored his first goal of the season three minutes and sixteen seconds into the game. In last year's N.C.A.A. final, in the Patriots' stadium, in Foxborough, Massachusetts, Cornell had a three-goal lead over Syracuse with four minutes to go, and apparently had the championship secured. But Syracuse exploded—one, two, three—and the game went into "sudden victory" overtime, the politically uplifting form of sudden death. Cornell got the overtime face-off and set up one of its shooting stars. He was going into a dodge when Sid Smith, of Syracuse, hit him with a clean check that dislodged the ball. Smith scooped it off the ground and began a clear that ended in the stick of Cody Jamieson, who released a shot so perfect that he did not watch it as it won the championship but ran instead sixty yards south to embrace his teammate Smith. Mohawks both, they had grown up together at Six Nations of the Grand River, an Iroquois reserve in Ontario.

Jamieson is of running-back size—five feet nine, two hundred and thirteen pounds—and out from under his helmet his look is boyish, his hair down his forehead in bangs. His elbows were heavily padded, his right leg was completely wrapped in some sort of therapeutic sleeve. His thighs and calves are massive, but they taper to a sprinter's ankles. His inside rolls resembled a spinning top. Eight and a half minutes into the game, he rolled right, dashed left, and scored again, unassisted. He would score four times. He wears 22, the number that Syracuse, in long tradition, has assigned each season to its best player.

Syracuse had a six-goal lead at the end of the first quarter, a nine-goal lead at the end of three. The starters retired. The final was 15–9. No one heckled the Denver coach.

Generally speaking, nobody beats Syracuse twice in one season. So if you lose to Syracuse you can dream about surprising them late. This Western team could come back East and get them in the Ravens' stadium, in Baltimore, in the N.C.A.A. tournament, in May. If not this May, some May.

Five years later, on May 23, 2015, in Philadelphia, Denver defeated Maryland for the national championship. This was not just Bill Tierney's seventh. He also became the only lacrosse coach ever to win the N.C.A.A. final at different universities. After watching the game on television, I sent him the most affectionate e-mail I could think of. All it said was "'Fuck you, coach!' Quote unquote."

Denver's Zach Miller, a sophomore who led the team in assists and was one of its three top scorers, had a pigtail running down his back and past his belt. Like some of the best players in modern lacrosse—in fact, the very best—Zach Miller is an Iroquois, a Seneca. He grew up on a reservation in northwestern New York. In a meeting with Tierney, when Miller was in high school, Miller's mother studied the coach's bristly, law-enforcing haircut, and asked him if he was going to make Zach cut off his pigtail. "No," said Tierney. "I may grow one."

Direct
Eye
Contact

FIFTY-FIVE YEARS AGO, I BUILT A HOUSE (THAT IS, paid for the building of it) in the northwest corner of Princeton Township, in New Jersey. It was on an unpaved road, running through woods and past an abandoned cornfield that had become a small meadow. My house looks out through trees and down that meadow.

Improbably, I developed a yearning, almost from the get-go, to see a bear someday in the meadow. While I flossed in the morning, looking north through an upstairs bathroom window, I hoped to see a bear come out of the trees. If this seems quixotic, it was. This was four miles from the campus of Princeton University, around which on all sides was what New Yorkers were calling a bedroom community. Deer were present in large familial groups, as they still are, but in even larger families. They don't give a damn about much of anything, and when I walk down the driveway in the morning to pick up the newspaper, I all but have to push them out of the way. Beforehand, of course, I have been upstairs flossing, looking down the meadow. No bears.

In 1966, in a conversation in Trenton with Lester Mac-Namara, the head of the state's Division of Fish and Game, I learned that there were twenty-two wild bears in New Jersey. Most lived on and near Kittatinny Mountain, in Sussex County, up the Delaware River. Sussex was once under a vertical kilometer of ice, and it looks it. It looks like Vermont. Kittatinny is actually a component of one very long mountain that runs, under various names, from Alabama to Newfoundland as the easternmost expression of the folded-and-faulted, deformed Appalachians. Through Sussex County, it carries the Appalachian Trail. New Jersey bears are best off there, and they know they are best off there, but they are as curious as they are hungry, and they range widely looking for mates. MacNamara happened to learn, while I was with him in his office, that a farmer in Pottersville had shot and killed a bear up a tree, and MacNamara, on his telephone, was shouting mad. Twenty-one.

Pottersville is in Hunterdon County, and Hunterdon is the next county to Mercer, and Mercer is where I am. In 1980, a bear came through Hunterdon and into Mercer, skirted Princeton, and somehow crossed U.S. 1 and I-195, five miles from the center of Trenton. In Yardville, a cop shot and killed it. New Jersey's bear biologists would have preferred to get there first, shoot the bear with Ketaset, put it in a pickup after it conked out, and take it to the Kittatinny before it woke up.

So please note: my ambition to see a bear in my backyard has not been completely insane. By the latest estimate, there are about twenty-five hundred bears in New Jersey now. Wild bears. Black bears. And perhaps not a few that have emigrated from Pennsylvania in search of a better life. In recent years, bears have been spotted in every New Jersey county.

Nassau Street is the main street of Princeton—town on one side, university on the other—and a bear has been seen on Nassau Street, close by the so-called "tree streets" (Chestnut, Walnut, Linden, Maple, Spruce, and Pine). I grew up on Maple Street. If I wanted to see a bear, I should have stayed put. Marshall Provost, a longtime friend of mine who recently left the Princeton police force to become a federal police officer in the District of Columbia, has told me that Princeton's official attitude toward bears is "Just leave them alone." He nonetheless investigated the Tree Street Bear. "I walked within ten feet of it. It was leaning against a tree." Of another bear, he said, "It was all over Princeton. That guy travelled." As did still another bear. Nick Sutter, the town's police chief, told me that it was seen at the Hun School and all over Princeton's Ascot-class neighborhoods—Elm Road, Constitution Hill—and on Chambers Street in the middle of town. Princeton's benign and respectful disposition toward wild bears is not in any way unusual or special in this exemplary state, whose municipalities, counties, and state agencies come on in choral unison about what to do when they show up in your backyard.

"Just let 'em go."

"Just leave 'em alone."

"Be cautious," said an online article from Lawrence Township

(Mercer County). "A black bear was spotted Sunday on Surrey Drive." In Laurel Run Village, a development in Bordentown (Burlington County), a bear stood up six feet tall, looked around, and went off into the woodlot next door.

Essex, New Jersey's second-densest county, with a population per square mile that outdenses the Netherlands, has had a number of recent sightings of wild black bears. On Memorial Day weekend, 2016, in West Caldwell, a bear was seen "in the area of Herbert Place and Eastern Parkway," according to a piece by Eric Kiefer on the website Patch. The bear, or another bear, next played Verona, "on Crestmont Road in the area of Claremont Ave." This was fourteen miles from the editorial offices of *The New Yorker*, which look out across the Hudson, over the Meadowlands, and far into Essex County.

In May, 2017, in Middletown Township (Monmouth County), bears were sighted on Nut Swamp Road and, a day later, on Packard Drive. In Manchester Township (Ocean County), a wild black bear went up a backyard tree in the neighborhood called Holly Oaks, where it tried to look like a black burl weighing two hundred and fifty pounds. According to a piece by Rob Spahr, of NJ Advance Media, "officers used sirens, air horns and water hoses to move the bear." The bear moved. Because it might return, police told residents, "Be vigilant." They also recommended that citizens review the bear-safety advice of, as it is called now, the state's Division of Fish and Wildlife, Department of Environmental Protection:

> Never feed or approach a bear! Remain calm if you
> encounter a bear. Make the bear aware of your presence
> by speaking in an assertive voice, singing, clapping your
> hands, or making other noises. Make sure the bear has

an escape route. If a bear enters your home, provide it with an escape route by propping all doors open. Avoid direct eye contact, which may be perceived by a bear as a challenge. Never run from a bear. Instead, slowly back away. To scare the bear away, make loud noises by yelling, banging on pans or using an air horn. Make yourself look as big as possible by waving your arms. If you are with someone else, stand close together with your arms raised above your head.

In the past three years, twenty-one bears have entered New Jersey homes, with no human fatalities. For example, Diane Eriksen, of West Milford (Passaic County), was under the impression that she was alone in her house. Hearing a sound in her living room, she went and had a look. A bear looked back. She beat a retreat and called 911. The bear, at the coffee table, helped itself to half a bowl of peppermint patties, scattered the wrappers all over the floor, and took off. The 911 call resulted in its death.

The state's advisory continues:

The bear may utter a series of huffs, make popping jaw sounds by snapping its jaws and swat the ground. These are warning signs that you are too close. Slowly back away, avoid direct eye contact and do not run. If a bear stands on its hind legs or moves closer, it may be trying to get a better view or detect scents in the air. It is usually not a threatening behavior. Black bears will sometimes "bluff charge" when cornered, threatened or attempting to steal food. Stand your ground, avoid direct eye contact, then slowly back away and do not run. If the bear does not leave, move to a secure area. Report black bear damage or nuisance behavior to the DEP's 24-hour, toll-free hotline at 1-877-WARN DEP (1-877-927-6337). Families who live in areas frequented by black bears should have a "Bear Plan" in place for children, with an escape route and planned use of whistles and air horns. Black bear attacks are extremely rare. If a black bear does attack, fight back.

To be sure, they are dangerous. Mistakenly described as "sedentary," even "harmless," they can be every bit as lethal as grizzlies. Years ago, a geologist I know lost both her arms to a black bear in Alaska's Yukon-Tanana terrain. In 2002, a bear in Sullivan County, New York, removed an infant from a stroller, carried her into the woods, and killed her. In 2014, a Rutgers student was killed by a bear in Passaic County, New Jersey. Horrible as such events are, bear stories gathering in the mind across time tend to exaggerate their own frequency. In the past twenty years, fourteen people in the United States have been killed by black bears. In 2012, one person killed twenty children in Connecticut. In 2018 . . .

POLICE IN THE Borough of Middlesex (Middlesex County) posted a Nixle notification: "Be alert, secure garbage and NEVER feed or approach bears." Lawrence Township told Lawrentians to bring garbage cans and bird feeders inside. Bordentown police went on Facebook to face down bears.

Evidently, there are fewer bears to face down than there were a year ago. Statewide, reported bear sightings dropped from seven hundred and twenty-two in 2016 to two hundred and sixty-three in 2017. Why this is so is not definitively known. With increased hunting, they have surely become warier. They could also have seen enough and gone back to the Poconos. But New Jersey bears are, of course, almost all native, and they are reproductively more fruitful than the nine hundred thousand black bears elsewhere in North America, whose average number of cubs per birth is a bit above two. The New Jersey average is 2.9. New Jersey sows have dropped as many as six cubs in a litter, and five, and four. New Jersey bears have a more concentrated forage of acorns, hazelnuts, beechnuts, and so forth—items that build fat. Fat equals health, and, in winter, nourishment for the mother making milk for her cubs, which are born in the den.

In 2003, New Jersey decided that its bear population had increased to a size that needed "management." Bear hunting, banned in 1971, was "reintroduced" and took place in early December, during deer season. In 2015, the bear-hunting season was greatly increased, with a new "segment," in October, when black bears are much more active, and the licensee was permitted to use a bow and arrow or a muzzleloader, the gun that fired the shot heard round the world. There are more muzzleloaders in the United States today than there were people in colonial America in 1775. In the late twentieth century, a muzzleloader in California ignited a fire that burned three thousand eight hundred and sixty acres. If something like that were not enough to make a bear wary, New Jersey's over-all "harvest" surely has been. In fifteen years, New Jersey hunters have killed four thousand bears. Among conjectures about the cause of the decline in bear sightings, that one seems prominent. The fact that New Jersey bears are "crepuscular"—that is, they move about before sunrise and after sunset, and spend the rest of the day in a swamp—has more to do with sheer intelligence than it does with nature. New Jersey's governor, Phil Murphy (Monmouth County), came into office declaring that he was going to ban the bear hunt once more.

In the past several decades, I have done most of my shad fishing on the upper Delaware River in Wayne County, Pennsylvania, opposite Sullivan County, New York. Pennsylvania estimates its population of black bears at twenty thousand, and a lot of them are in Wayne County, where I have never seen one, but they are around us all the time. In a storm, a big oak in mast, up a slope from my cabin there, fell not long ago. Its trunk broke freakishly—about twenty feet up—and the crown bent all the way over and spread the upper branches like a broom upon the ground. In the branches were a number of thousands of acorns. The next morning, enough bear shit was around that oak to fertilize the Philadelphia Flower Show. But nary a bear. A neighbor, though, went around a corner of his cabin one day and almost bumped into a bear coming the other way. The bear was so afraid of this neighbor that it turned, ran down the bank to the river, jumped in, and swam to New York. Black bears are strong swimmers.

My ambition to see one in my own backyard came extremely close to success on the eleventh of August, 2016. My wife, Yolanda Whitman, was sitting in the living room and happened to look up. A bear came out of the trees and started across the meadow. And where was I at this milestone of a moment? I was in a basement recording studio in a new building on the Princeton campus, making a podcast about Princeton basketball with Mitch Henderson, the head coach.

My résumé remains empty. Looking down from our windows, I have never seen a bear. Mitch Henderson will have to do. Meanwhile, as Yolanda watched, the bear reached mid-meadow and sat down. This was not before sunrise or after sunset. This was late morning. This bear was not afraid of anything. Rolling its shoulders, flexing, shrugging, soaking up the sun, it groomed itself. It sat there and groomed itself (!!!), while I, talking to Mitch, was in a cellar designed by Frank Gehry, and Yolanda, whose mind is full of presence, was taking pictures of the bear.

Part II

An
Album
Quilt

IN AN ALBUM QUILT, the blocks differ, each from all the others. The passages that follow here seem to call for such a title. They are taken from writing I have done that has not previously appeared in any book. Getting this project under way, I looked through pieces written for both public and private occasions through the years, and selected a passage here and there. These included a number of short *New Yorker* pieces, and stories of varied length from other magazines and from *Time*, where I worked before I joined *The New Yorker*. I looked through some dozens of things I wrote when I was in college, and threw them all out. In aggregate, I sifted about two hundred and fifty thousand words and got rid of seventy-five per cent. I didn't aim to reprint the whole of anything. Instead, I was looking for blocks to add to the quilt, and not without new touches, internal deletions, or changed tenses—trying to make something, not just preserve it, and hoping the result would be engaging to read.

With fifty-six three-by-five cards on a large smooth table, I reached an arrangement of passages in an intentionally various, random, and subjective manner. I meant that they should be read that way—all at once, or, say, half a dozen pages after a crack of the book.

DESIGNER'S NOTE: The crossed-canoe blocks on this and the following pages are from a paper pieced quilt made by Cass Garner, of Stockton, New Jersey, as a gift to John McPhee.

An
Album
Quilt

CARY GRANT HAS VIRTUALLY EVERY NICKEL HE HAS EVER earned. He was once seen handing a few coins to his wife and counting them first. After the Plaza Hotel sent him one and a half English muffins for breakfast, he called the head of room service and the manager and even threatened to call Conrad Hilton, the owner, claiming that the menu said "muffins" and a measly one and a half did not live up to the plural.

Lean, suave, incomparably tanned, he never wears makeup and, across time, has become steadily better-looking. More or less successfully, he spends his real life pretending he is Cary

Grant. Open *Paris Match*, for example, and there, in all likelihood, will be a picture of him in an Italian car, zooming east of Nice on the Moyenne Corniche—the route he followed with Grace Kelly in *To Catch a Thief.* He is the darling of the internationals, a janissary in Kelly's Monegasque toy palace, a captive treasure among the potentates and popinjays of the Onassis floating salon.

Being Cary Grant is such a gilded role that all sorts of other people think they are Cary Grant, too. Tony Curtis, for example, seems to caricature Grant in everything he does. He dresses like Grant, but with tighter trousers; his accent seems to be an attempt to sound like Grant; and he imitates Grant on the screen. When Curtis bought a Rolls-Royce, he made sure he got a better one than Grant's.

Grant has many apes but few friends. In Hollywood—he has a mansion in Beverly Hills—he runs with no pack and is rarely seen at parties or premieres. The director Billy Wilder recently said, "I don't know anyone who has been to Grant's house in the last ten years." Grant steadfastly insists that he has as much right to privacy as a plumber or a municipal clerk. When people ask for his autograph, he gives them an incredulous look as if they are trying to crash a party, and if some jolly clod says, "Put your John Hancock right here, Cary," he says, "My name is not John Hancock, and I have no intention of putting it anywhere." On one occasion, a rebuffed fan snapped, "Who the hell do you think you are?" Cool as the north wind, Grant answered, "I know who I am. I haven't the vaguest idea who you are, and furthermore I don't care to know."

Cary Grant, of course, is Archibald Alexander Leach ("My name will give you an idea what kind of family I came from"), son of a textile worker in provincial Britain. When Archie was twelve, his father deserted his mother, a tall and commanding woman who for a time went to pieces under the shock of rejection. Little Archie, essentially homeless, turned to show business and ran away to join a troupe of acrobats.

Perhaps reacting to his dark-haired, dark-eyed mother, he has had three blond, blue-eyed wives. The first was Virginia Cherrill, the flower girl in Charlie Chaplin's *City Lights*; the second was the Woolworth heiress Barbara Hutton (unlike her other husbands, Grant did not ask for alimony); the third was the actress Betsy Drake, whose grandfather built the Drake and Blackstone hotels in Chicago. An accomplished hypnotist, Drake put Grant to sleep at various times and helped him to stop smoking and drinking. Together they explored Asian religions, transcendentalism, mysticism, and yoga. Grant claims that through her he learned how to put one side of his jaw to sleep when a dentist happened to be drilling there. For years, they were intimately estranged, living apart, dating each other frequently, taking trips together. Once, at a Broadway show, Cary saw her come in with another man. "There's my wife," he said to his own companion. "Isn't she beautiful?"

Grant and his psychiatrist tried using LSD to help uproot Cary's deepest psychological problems. Often called instant analysis, LSD is said to clean out the subconscious like lye in a septic tank. Impressed by his own progress under its influence, Grant delivered a confessional lecture at U.C.L.A. "I was a self-centered boor," he told the fascinated students. "I was masochistic and only thought I was happy. When I woke up and said, 'There must be something wrong with me,' I grew up." In a subsequent interview, he went on to say, "Because I never understood myself, how could I have hoped to understand anyone else? That's why I say that now I can truly give a woman

love for the first time in my life, because I can understand her."
Last week, Betsy Drake filed for divorce.

On a set, he drives directors and fellow actors round the bend with his fussy attention to minutiae. He once went over the scalps of innumerable extras to see if their hair had been properly dyed. While filming *That Touch of Mink*, with Doris Day, he went shopping with her and supervised her purchase of shoes, skirts, and blouses to wear in the picture. On the movie lot, he was so disturbed when he saw the paintings on a set wall that he held up production while he went home and returned with better ones from his private collection. "A thousand details add up to one impression," he explained.

In his studio office are very large photographs of all his wives, and numberless mementos of his long and lofty career. "The good old days are now," he says, grinning amiably. An editor, checking facts, recently sent a telegram to him, asking, "HOW OLD CARY GRANT?" He wired back, "OLD CARY GRANT FINE. HOW YOU?"

IN THE SPORT AND CAMPING SHOW at the New York Coliseum, a former Ping-Pong champion of the United States, Great Britain, Canada, and South America played Ping-Pong with Mrs. John Lindsay, the First Lady of the City of New York, who bobbed gracefully about, hitting sweeping ground strokes in response to the champion's steady game. "Hi, Mrs. Lindsay!" a voice called from the crowd outside the picket fence surrounding the playing area. "Call me Mary," said Mary, without taking her eye off the ball. The professional sent up a high, dizzy lob that seemed to come down like a falling leaf. "Ooo!" said Mary. "Show me that one again. I want to try it on my children." After offering another lob, the pro, with some insolence, began to answer her volleys by raising one leg and hitting the ball with the bottom of his foot. Mrs. Lindsay watched for her chance, and sent a baseline drive whistling past him while his leg waved absurdly in the air.

A professional pool player prepared to demonstrate trick shots. An announcer with a small, intimate loudspeaker told the crowd that the professional would begin by sinking three balls at once. The pro chalked up and tried the shot. The cue ball rocketed into the three setups, and the balls dispersed to various cushions, but not one dropped into a pocket. He tried again. He missed again. He tried again. He missed again. "I don't think this table is quite right," said the announcer, who was—at least until that moment—an employee of the manufacturer of the table.

Oscar Robertson, of basketball's Cincinnati Royals, entered the hall and was immediately surrounded by at least two thousand people, more than half of them adults. To get near him, they climbed over booths, broke down barricades, and temporarily paralyzed most of the exhibits in the show. National Shoes had engaged Robertson to make an appearance and sign autographs. Soon, Robertson was standing in a small "basketball court"—ten feet wide by twenty feet long—between a pair of backboards made of thin composition board and equipped with attached hoops of the sort that are sold in dime stores. The crowd seemed to surge like a throng in Saint Peter's Square. A little boy, perhaps ten years old, stood beside Robertson, and Robertson handed him a basketball. The boy took a shot, and missed. Robertson retrieved the ball and handed it to him again. The boy shot again, and missed. Robertson leaned down and talked to the boy. Not just a word or two. He spoke into the boy's ear for half a minute. The boy shot again. Swish. Robertson himself seemed reluctant to try a shot. The baskets were terrible, and—even if they had not been—a basketball player makes only about half his shots anyway. A few misses, and this crowd really would not have understood. Moreover, Robertson was wearing an ordinary business suit, so his movements would be restricted. He signed a few autographs. "Shoot, Big O!" someone called out. Others took up the cry. "Shoot, Big O!" Robertson turned aside, and signed another autograph. "Shoot, Big O!" Robertson studied one of the baskets. This might have been a mistake, because there was no retreating now. Once a basketball player, with a ball in his hand, looks up at a basket, almost nothing can make him resist the temptation to take a shot. Robertson stepped back to a point about seventeen feet from the basket and lifted the ball high, and a long set shot rolled off his fingers and began to arc toward the basket with a slow backspin. The crowd was suddenly quiet. Everybody watched the ball except Robertson, whose eyes never left the basket until the ball had dropped in. He shot again. Swish. Again. Swish. Five, six, seven in a row. There was no one else in the Coliseum now. Robertson—making set shots, jump shots, even long, graceful hook shots—had retreated from the crowd into the refuge of his talent.

THE TILT of these essentially parallel faults is to the north. In each earthquake, the lower side slipped north, the upper side moved south. In each earthquake, the north-south dimension of the basin shortened somewhat, and its adjacent mountains went up a couple of feet. This local compression began in relatively recent time, when the Pacific Lithospheric Plate, moving essentially northward, sort of shouldered into the North American Plate where the San Andreas Fault presents an awkward curve that is known in geology as a prominent restraining bend. The mountains went up. People came, and Los Angeles went up. The mountains, hills, anticlines will continue to go up, the basin will continue to be compressed, as long as the Pacific Plate keeps pushing into the restraining bend. The Pacific Plate, sliding, weighs three hundred and forty-five quadrillion tons.

Like a city planner, the plate motions have created Los Angeles. The plate motions have shaped its setting and its setting's exceptional beauty, raising its intimate mountains ten thousand feet. The mountains are such a phalanx that air flowing in from the west cannot get over them, and a result is the inversion layer that concentrates smog. Plate motions in Los Angeles folded the anticlines that trapped the oil that rained gold and silver into the streets. Plate motions have formed a basin so dry that water must be carried to it five hundred miles. Plate motions have built the topography that has induced the weather that has brought the fire that has prepared the topography for city-wrecking flows of rock debris. Plate motions are benign, fatal, eternal, causal, beneficial, ruinous, continual, and inevitable. It's all in the luck of the cards. Plate motions are earthquakes.

IN AN OLD NEW ENGLAND HOUSE, Eric Sloane found a wood-backed, leather-bound diary written in 1805 by a fifteen-year-old boy. Its entries were terse: "June 3—Helped Father build rope hoist to move the water wheel," or "June 26—Father and I sledded the oaks from the woodlot and put them down near the mill." Sloane took the diary and dressed it out with verbal and graphic sketches, detailing the construction of a whole backwoods farm. Mere antiquity is not what interests him. Instead, he puts a shine and an edge on the tools of the pioneers, constantly admiring the care and skill of craftsmen who thought enough of themselves, their work, and the times they lived in to date and sign everything they made.

Sloane shows how to build a house without a nail in it that will go up and stay up for hundreds of years, how to make a bottle-glass window, a fieldstone grike, a folding ladder, a wooden tub, a cider press. Two ways to stack cordwood. A recipe for brown ink ("Boiled down walnut or butternut hulls that have been mashed first. Add vinegar and salt to boiling water to 'set'"). From king posts to roofing, he details the construction of a covered bridge, which was an 1805 innovation. George Washington never saw one.

The mill wheel was the all-purpose appliance that could run saws, pump bellows, grind grain, keep trip hammers thumping, turn meat spits, and rock babies—all at once. Woods were selected according to capability, and when a wagon was built—oak frame, elm sides and floor, ash spokes and shafts, pine seat, hickory slats—it lasted about twelve times as long as a Cadillac does now.

Young boys, like the one whose diary Sloane follows, would get up on winter mornings, run across the road to the barn, push the cow or ox aside, then stand and dress in the warm area where the animal had been sleeping. If a house had more than ten panes of glass, the owner paid a glass tax—so most houses had ten and no more. Window glass, in fact, was so valuable that a family often took the panes with them when they moved from one house to another. If a woman died, the church bell tolled six times. A man was worth nine. Then, after a pause, the exact age of the late member of the congregation was tintinnabulated for all to note. If a family had a bridge on their land, they charged neighbors and strangers a toll to cross it. (This was a tradition that time would honor. Until 1955, for example, a suspension bridge more than a mile long, crossing part of Narragansett Bay, was the private property of Rudolf Haffenreffer, who gathered more than a million a year in tolls.)

In a time when two-car garages have phony haylofts and cocktails rest on cobblers' benches, the ways of the early Americans are more often exploited than understood. Sloane understands them. When he closes his hand around the handle of an old wooden tool, he says, he can all but feel "the very hand that wore it smooth." He hands the tool to his reader.

I PARKED MY FORD in lower Manhattan, locked it, went about some business, and returned to find that I had left the key inside. Damn. Every window was shut tight. The nearest duplicate key, as it happened, was a fifty-dollar cab ride away, in New Jersey. The parking space was under an elevated segment of the Franklin D. Roosevelt Drive, in a moted half-light that swiftly lost what little magic it had had, and turned to condensed gloom. Trash barrels were spaced among the steel supports of the highway. Refuse was all over the ground. I searched the area and rummaged through one barrel after another, looking for wire.

Finally, in a mass of broken Gallo bottles, I found the classic tool of the car thief—a metal coat hanger. Unfortunately, I lacked the skill to use it. I knew, in a general way, the technique. Make the coat hanger into a straight piece of wire, then bend it so that it's like a big hairpin, then twist one end to form a hook. Work the wire in past the rubber that rims a window. Now maneuver the hook down the inside and—most adroit move of all—get a grip on the lock button. Firmly, slowly, lift the wire. Sesame.

I poked around my nondescript car looking for a spot soft enough to penetrate, and did not meet with early success. I jabbed for a while at the windows on one side, then moved around the car. Finally, I got the wire in about two inches, but beyond that it was reluctant to move. While I was shoving at it, a car pulled up beside me, and I noticed from the corner of my eye the familiar green and black of a sedan of the police of the City of New York. Two policemen were inside. I pulled out the wire, waved it at them, and said, "Hello. Hi. The key is locked inside, you see, and . . ."

The policemen got out of the patrol car, and one of them asked for the wire. I handed it to him. He stuck it into the Ford like a baker testing a cake. In three seconds, perhaps less, he had the car door standing open. He returned the wire, and I thanked him.

The other policeman said to him, "Now give the lecture, Sam."

Sam gave a recitation on the foolhardiness of locking a key in a car.

Then the two policemen got back into their own vehicle and prepared to drive away.

"Wait," I said.

They had asked for no papers, no identification of any kind.

They had found me trying to insert a wire into a Ford. Were they just going to assume that the car was mine?

Sam, hearing all this, looked at his partner, then back at me. He said, "Listen, mister, if you're stealing that car, and you had the chutzpah to get us to help you, take it. It's yours. You can have it."

WITH HIS COLLABORATOR, Richard Rodgers, Oscar Hammerstein set a new standard for the modern musical play, integrating verse with dialogue, music with plot, in a theatrical form that once demanded little more than a loose collection of songs, skits, and dances. Hammerstein's lyrics were almost always written first, often completed after weeks of agony, walking mile upon mile on the blacktop roads near his Pennsylvania farm, using dummy tunes of his own invention to coax his words along toward a completed lyric. Hearing some of these mock-up melodies, Richard Rodgers staggered backward in amused horror. Whether Hammerstein was writing about Austrian singers, New England factory workers, or a Siamese king, there was always a steady undertone of old-fashioned optimism in his lyrics. He said, "I just can't write anything without hope in it." In 1943, when wartime headlines were black with death on coral beaches, *Oklahoma!* opened on Broadway, and Hammerstein's words carried across the world the picture of a beautiful morning, "a bright golden haze on the meadow." Just then, many people everywhere were grateful for the reminder that such a thing existed.

To people who grew up in the forties and fifties, humming

and dancing in the glow of Rodgers and Hammerstein, it sometimes came as a surprise that Hammerstein had an earlier, equally prodigious career in the operettas of the twenties. Before he turned thirty-five, he had written the lyrics of *Rose-Marie, The Desert Song, The New Moon*, and *Show Boat*. Introducing himself with such songs as "Indian Love Call" and "Stouthearted Men," he secured his position with "Ol' Man River."

He had many collaborators, and from them learned his craft. Otto Harbach, with whom Hammerstein worked on *The Desert Song*, taught him the basics of writing for the musical stage. Sigmund Romberg, confining his highest praise to the words "It fits, it fits," taught him the virtues of a sixteen-hour workday. Jerome Kern, who gave him the tall captain's table on which Hammerstein thereafter wrote standing up, taught him—ordered him, rather—never to use the word "Cupid" in a lyric. After hearing Kern's next melody for *Show Boat* (the music came first with Jerome Kern; words were filled in later), Hammerstein fired back lyrics that began:

Cupid knows the way,
He's the naked boy
Who can make you sway . . .

When Kern recovered, he was given an alternative:

Why do I love you?
Why do you love me?
Why should there be two
Happy as we?

From his home in Bronxville, Kern would call up Hammerstein in Great Neck, Long Island; then he would set the phone on his piano and bang away at the keyboard while the greatest American operetta grew along the wires. Although the Kerns and the Hammersteins were close friends, Hammerstein's wife, Dorothy, could not abide hearing people refer to "Jerome Kern's 'Ol' Man River.'" She would say to them, "Oscar Hammerstein wrote 'Ol' Man River.' Jerome Kern wrote Ta-ta dumdum, Ta ta-ta dumdum."

I HAVE WORKED for twenty years in East Pyne Hall at Princeton, in a corridor dominated by the Department of Comparative Literature, where the Council of the Humanities has a small inholding. Comp Lit has had two chairmen in its history at Princeton: Robert Fagles, whose translation of Homer is a work still in progress, and Robert Hollander, a curator of Dante. As both are overly fond of saying, I am an interloper there, a fake professor, a portfolio without minister. For all that, the third floor of East Pyne is a superb place to work. By six-thirty in the evening, it is essentially vacant. Even the tenure track is quietly rusting. At seven-thirty in the morning, though, a lonely figure will be wandering the hall—the back arched, the head a little cocked, the lips in perpetual motion—mumbling about warriors armed in bronze. Fagles understands bronze. Anyone with that much brass would understand bronze. Long ago I learned that if you hear him coming and you step into the corridor and confront him with a question, he turns into an ambulatory checking department, a mine of antique material, the willing donor in an act of cerebral osmosis. For example, there came a time when my geological compositions became focused on a passage about the island of Cyprus. I heard him coming, stepped into the hall, and later went back to my machine and wrote: "In 2760 B.C., smelting began in Cyprus. Slag heaps developed in forty places. The *Iliad* is populated with warriors armed in bronze. Bronze is copper hardened by adding some tin, and the copper would have come from Cyprus. (Copper was mined on Cyprus for nearly two thousand years before Homer.) . . . The word 'Cyprus' means copper. Whether the island is named for the metal or the metal for the island is an etymology lost in time."

When I bring Fagles fish from the Delaware River, as I sometimes do, he asks that they be gutted, finned, and scaled, and wrapped in my work.

I HAVE A FRIEND in Washington who knows the city from the inside in. H. M. Remeor is not his name, but it will do. He is of the category of people who have put in time feeding pens to Presidents and have long since melded into the panelling of D.C. law firms, where, although they have no specific connection with the government, they operate within a distinct aurora of clout. Remeor's Washington is not the Washington of Capital City Tours. For example, he once showed me through the cassette library in the Washington telephone exchange. He lives in the hills of suburban Maryland. In that general area, one autumn day, I was riding with him in his car when he turned into what appeared to be someone's long driveway. Wide lawns reached away from the drive, which ran between rows of deciduous trees and led to a large stone house. The day was cold but sunlit, and windy. Behind the house were a couple of dozen cars, parked in an ovate ring. Remeor drove into the middle of this circle, stopped, and said, "This is the parking lot at Burning Tree. That is the clubhouse. The golf course is over there. The course is hardly noticeable unless you get right on it. This place is so anonymous you'd never know it was here, but it precedes the Pentagon on Brezhnev's list of pinpoint targets in the Washington area. There are big men here, with big handicaps. More power goes off the tees of Burning Tree—for less distance—than at any other golf club on earth. Look who's here even on a day as cold as this."

I looked around and saw no one.

Remeor said, "Take a good look at the cars."

Directly in front of us was a Mercedes-Benz with an Arkansas license plate—MS 2.

"Member of the Senate, two," explained Remeor. "James William Fulbright, the junior senator from Arkansas. Naturally, he has a foreign car. He's the chairman of the Foreign Relations Committee."

Our eyes began to move from automobile to automobile, plate to plate: Thunderbird. Missouri—8.

"Now, who do you suppose that is?" Mr. Remeor said. "Who would you say is the eighth-most-important person in Missouri?"

I counted down my own list—the chairman of the board of Ralston Purina, Harry Truman, Governor Hearnes, Warren Bradley, Busch, Anheuser . . . "Symington," I said, finally. "Stuart Symington. Missouri 8."

"You've got it," Remeor said. "Now have a look at that one." He nodded toward a big Chrysler with a Maine license plate that had no numerals at all—just the word "SENATE," in large block letters.

"Muskie," I said.

"There can be no doubt of it. One thing for dead certain is that Margaret Chase Smith is not out here on this golf course today. Women are forbidden at Burning Tree. No woman ever sets foot in that clubhouse. A long time ago, Joe Davies offered to build and pay for a swimming pool here, and the offer was indignantly refused, on the ground that a pool would increase pressure from women and children. The members take considerable pride in the fact that they can walk around nude in any part of the building."

I wondered how well everyone was doing on the golf course on such a cold afternoon, and from my home in New Jersey some days later I would call up the cars' owners to find out. Senator Symington, for example, said that the temperature had discouraged him, so he had just hit some balls from the practice tee. Senator Muskie's office told me that Muskie had played and then had gone off to Moscow. "The Senator is very modest about his golf game, with good reason," said a member of his staff, who went on to say that three years ago, in Kennebunk, Muskie had made a hole in one, and that he breaks 90 with about the same frequency.

Senator Fulbright described his golf game in a general way, and there was something in his manner that might have suggested—had I been less familiar with the probity of the source—the crafted self-deprecation of an organized hustler. "My game is pretty poor," he said. "I don't play enough. I'm getting old and decrepit. There's nothing very exciting about my golf game or about the life I lead. As we get older, we get progressively duller and duller—you'll find that out. I used to play more, but ever since I've been the chairman of the committee I haven't been in the seventies. My golf is very poor. I played lacrosse at Oxford in 1926, and, before that, football at Arkansas. I injured my knees very badly. The cartilage is out. That hampers my golf. I didn't have a scheduled match. I just went out that afternoon and picked up a game."

The game he picked up was J. Lawn Thompson, M.D. (District of Columbia, Thunderbird—701), physician to Cabinets and Congresses, and former curator of Lyndon B. Johnson.

"Hello, Dr. Thompson. How did you fare on the golf course with Senator Fulbright the other day?"

"As usual, I was talked out of everything. Senator Fulbright is a very persuasive man, not only in national politics but on the first tee. He has a way of creating unjustified sympathy for himself. He tells you how hard he's been working, you know, and how tired he is, and that he hasn't played golf very much, and the next thing you know you're giving him strokes when he should be giving you strokes. So that's how I fared. I reached in my pocket and paid him all of my Medicare fees for the past month."

"What was your score, Dr. Thompson?"

"Eighty-four."

"What was the Senator's score?"

"Three shots less—just enough, you know, to hang me up on the wall."

I would also try a call to the office of Senator Smith, for it nagged me that Muskie's license plate merely said "SENATE." What, then, could hers possibly say? "It says '1,'" said her administrative assistant.

Moving slowly through the parking lot, Mr. Remeor next pointed out a Florida Lincoln Continental—MC 9.

"Member of Congress, Ninth District," I said.

"You're ready," he said. "Paul Rogers, of West Palm Beach, is the Congressman from the Ninth District of Florida."

Ohio, Continental—FMF. "That's a tough one," Remeor said. "Unless you happen to know that Congressman Michael A. Feighan, of Ohio, once married a girl named Florence Mathews."

District of Columbia, Mercury—341. "That's Doug Mode," Remeor said. "He's a lawyer. Does the same sort of thing I do. Doug was a pallbearer at Walter Hagen's funeral, and he has a set of Hagen's clubs, but he's not much of a golfer. He plays golf in the fall, when there are no gnats. Today, he'll be in there playing gin. He was the advance man for Dewey in the '44 campaign."

I asked Mr. Remeor if he himself was a golfer.

"Oh, Lord, no," he said. "I can't stand the game."

Passing by a Mercedes-Benz, DPL 2079 (D.C. plate), Remeor said, "Luis Machado. Note the diplomatic license. He was once the Cuban Ambassador to the United States. Before that, he was president of the Havana Country Club."

Cadillac, D.C.—144. "You know Abe Fortas's old law firm, Arnold, Fortas & Porter?" Remeor said. "Well, that's Porter. Porter has a chauffeur named Henry Ford."

One automobile at Burning Tree—a Continental, Texas, BKZ 922—attracted us not because of its license number but because of its size. There was something magnified about it. It seemed too big for a continent, let alone a Continental. Each of its fenders appeared to be large enough to garage a Volkswagen.

Surely all this automobile could not be the carapace of a mere Senator. Mr. Remeor had no idea whose it was, so I later called a policeman friend and he radioed somewhere and word came quickly back that Texas BKZ 922 was the automobile of Lieutenant General John C. Meyer, Director of Operations, United States Air Force, two hundred combat missions over Europe, one of the top air aces of all time, Croix de Guerre from France and Belgium, Air Medal, Silver Star, D.F.C., and D.S.C., with thirteen (Did you say thirteen? Roger. Repeat, thirteen) oak-leaf clusters. I put in a call to the Pentagon, and soon sensed just how big a general General Meyer is, for in order to propose a talk with him I had to spend fifteen minutes talking with another general—Brigadier General H. L. Hogan III (five oak-leaf clusters)—who politely told me that he would see what he could do, and would call me back. A day or so later, he called to say that he was still having difficulty getting through to General Meyer on the matter of the golf game but that he would continue the effort and call me again. "I just didn't want you to think we weren't working on the problem," said generous General Hogan. "Let's see what we can whomp up." Two days later, the Pentagon called again. "This is General Hogan," said General Hogan. "Stand by for General Meyer!"

"This is General Meyer speaking. My game is generally pretty bad. I must have played a lousy game that afternoon, because if it was good I would remember the score. I played with two other generals. We didn't find the weather particularly cold. I would guess I was somewhere around my usual game, which is like ninety-two or three or four. If I was worse than a hundred, I would remember that, too. If I'd played a good game, I could tell you every stroke."

At Burning Tree, as we retreated down the long driveway, Mr. Remeor said, "You may recall that Burning Tree is where the Martian landed on the eighth green and went up to President Eisenhower and said, 'Take me to your leader.' This place has a rich history. The policy of the club has always been that it wants no publicity whatsoever, but sometimes it can't help getting it. According to another story that went around, Ike was playing here one day and Secret Service men came running out of the woods and conferred with him, and then they rushed up the fairway to the next foursome and said, 'Excuse us, gentlemen, but do you mind if the President plays through? We have just received word that New York has been bombed.' . . . Yes, yes, Nixon is a member here. The President and the Vice President—Nixon and Agnew. They've even got the president of the P.G.A. in there, as their pro. Of all the American Presidents who have ever played the game, John Kennedy was by a country mile the best golfer. His back bothered him, and he played for only a short period each time he came out here. He would just show up, shoot a few pars, and leave. Think of this: Nixon sponsored John Kennedy for membership here. The club has a collection of drivers that have been used by Presidents. By and large, the members are an informal and unstuffy bunch of men. In the summertime, they play in short pants and wear no shirts. Some of them play in their undershorts. They put on long drawers and play all through the winter. I've been in clubs all over the world that have big mazumbos in their membership, and this one is the least pretentious, the most homey, the most humble. There is nothing burning here. Centuries ago, there was a tree here that glowed in the night, probably from phosphorus, so the Indians called this region Potomac, the Place of the Burning Tree."

HER FEET ARE TOO BIG. Her nose is too long. Her teeth are uneven. She has the neck, as one of her rivals has put it, of "a Neapolitan giraffe." Her waist seems to begin in the middle of her thighs, and she has big, half-bushel hips. She runs like a fullback. Her hands are huge. Her forehead is low. Her mouth is too large. And, *mamma mia*, she is absolutely gorgeous.

By her own description, Sophia Loren is "a unity of many irregularities." She has rewritten the canons of beauty. A daughter of the Bay of Naples, she has within her the blood of the Saracens, Spanish, Normans, Byzantines, and Greeks. The East appears in her slanting eyes. Her dark brown hair is a bazaar of rare silk. Her legs talk. In her impish, ribald Neapolitan laughter, she epitomizes the Capriccio Italien that Tchaikovsky must have had in mind. Lord Byron, in her honor, probably sits up in his grave about once a week and rededicates his homage to "Italia! oh, Italia! thou who hast the fatal gift of beauty." *Vogue* magazine once fell to its skinny knees and abjectly admitted: "After Loren, bones are boring." Catherine de Medici decreed that women should strive for a waist measurement of 13 inches. Sophia Loren sets the template now: 38-24-38. She is what the Spanish call "much woman" and the French "*une femme plantureuse*." Italians once called Gina Lollobrigida "La Gina Nazionale." They now call Sophia Loren "La Sophia Seducente." They prefer the seductress. Gina was, in their curious view, too refined. Sophia, they say, is a woman of the people, their *donna popolana*.

Her body is a mobile of miscellaneous fruits and melons, and her early career was largely a matter of putting them on display. But

Sophia no longer leans forward for just any passing Leica. "Some-day," she says with the earnestness of a starlet, "I hope that every-one will say I am a great actress and I will be remembered for that."

(She won the Academy Award for Best Actress, in 1962, for *Two Women*.)

Pozzuoli, on the Bay of Naples, where Sophia grew up, has been described in a travel book as "perhaps the most squalid city in Italy." The most squalid city in Italy has music in its streets, cluttered pink-and-white buildings, seagulls screaming over-head, a bright blue waterfront, a Roman amphitheatre where Gennaro—the patron saint of Naples—achieved his exaltation simply because a pride of lions refused to eat him. It now has a municipal slogan: "What a woman we have exported."

Little Sofia—the "ph" was inserted later because it seems more exotic to the Italian eye—was turned over to a hired wet nurse after her mother's breasts went dry as a consequence of poor health. From a bed swarming with six grandchildren, the wet nurse last week reminisced: "Sophia was the ugliest child I ever saw in my life. She was so ugly that I am sure no one else would have wanted to give her milk. It was my milk that made Sophia beautiful, and now she doesn't even remember me. I gave milk to hundreds of children, but none of them drank as much as Sophia. Her mother gave me fifty lire a month. Sophia drank at least a hundred lire worth of milk. Madonna *mia!*"

Schoolmates scrawled on the door of her house the word *stecchetto* (little stick), because she was as thin as one. At four-teen, the little stick suddenly blossomed. Gymnastics classes were held in the Roman amphitheatre, and the men of Pozzuoli began to show up to watch Sophia doing calisthenics. "It be-came a pleasure just to stroll down the street," Sophia remem-bers. Mamma had thought that Sophia should try to become a teacher, but she took another look and put her in a beauty contest. In the spring of 1950, mother and daughter went off to Rome to seek work in films. "There I told my first big lie for Sophia," her mother says. "Someone called out, 'This way for girls who speak English.' 'Sure,' I told the man, 'my daughter speaks English. Don't you speak English, Sophia?'

"'*Si*, Mamma.'"

IN THE MOSCOW STATE CIRCUS there are no elephants. No tigers. No lions. No giraffes. No orangutans. Bears.

Big bears. Little bears. Black bears. Brown bears. Mamma bears. Great strong hammer-sickle thick-coated rocket-powered Soviet bears. Trained by Valentin Filatov on a third of a ton of lump sugar a day, they roller-skate, ride bicycles and scooters, and hang from whirling trapezes. Three of them draw a troika. Two of them fight, wearing boxing gloves. They hook and jab. They drive motorcycles in the dark, turning the headlights on and off and stopping for traffic lights along the way. They're so intelligent they're painful to watch, because they make an American think of all those snobbish, slobbish fat brown blubber-bottomed freeloading Yellowstone bears, who have yet to lift a claw for their country.

ONE SUMMER in the nineteen-fifties, the editorial staff of *Time* began to collect material for a cover story about Americans on holiday. Boris Chaliapin, who had produced more *Time* cover pictures than any other artist, was asked to create a work expressing the theme. The resulting picture was not used. It was consigned to darkness with the fatal term "NR" ("not running"). Chaliapin had painted the Statue of Liberty on water skis. Her robes had been shed on Bedloe's Island and were draped there over her plinth. She now wore a bathing suit. Torch in hand, she scudded across the harbor.

I remembered that painting (who could ever forget it?), having seen it once, long ago in *Time*'s editorial offices in Rockefeller Center, when I worked there. It had been the star of a collection of analogous works, which had been commissioned and completed but, for one reason or another, had never seen the light of print—a gallery's worth of NR *Time* covers under dust in an outsize closet. Wondering how the collection had evolved in the intervening years, I called up Henry Grunwald, my former editor, now *Time*'s managing editor, and asked him.

Unused cover paintings and cover sculptures had a tendency to disappear, he said, but there was no lack of them on hand. He happened to have one, by Larry Rivers, on his own wall. It showed God lying in a coffin.

"Whose idea was that?"

"Larry Rivers's."

"May I look at it?"

"You may."

"And the others?"

"Why not?"

Grunwald is a courtly man, born and raised in Vienna, educated in New York, and he has an accent that lilts at all volumes. I found him sitting at his desk, twenty-five stories up. Framed by a window behind him, he himself might have been an NR cover of Henry Kissinger—the rippling hair, the middling height, the eyes that seemed to inflate behind glasses that had dark rims. The resemblance between the two men is considerable, and it is flattering to each to say that he looks like the other. Grunwald wore a striped tie and a brown-and-white striped shirt. He was managing his magazine through an intercom console that had many levers. As he went on speaking to genies all around the building, he waved hello and pointed to the wall where God lay dead.

The picture was a collage. God's coffin was a foldout affair, as if from a children's book, and an arrow that led away from the bier seemed to suggest a route by which He might escape. Subordinate themes surrounded the central image—sets of pictures and symbols having to do, apparently, with functions that in some way people had wrested from God. Medicine. Weather. Dishwashers. Rockets. Very, very subtle. Da Vinci's God had been pasted in and then, with a red crayon, crossed out. Rivers's God seemed in no hurry to get out of the coffin. All this had been too complex for the magazine, Grunwald told me. NR. Rivers had done the collage to accompany a cover story titled "Is God Dead?," and those words alone ran on the cover of the magazine, in red letters on a solid black field—the first time ever that the magazine had not used some sort of picture.

Larry Rivers had another cover in the NR collection, Grunwald told me. It had been an attempt to paste together the essence of Norman Mailer. In two rooms nearby, several dozen NR'd pictures, collages, and sculptures had been set out for viewing, and in one corner was Rivers's Mailer, coming apart in layers. Rivers had started with a photograph of his subject's face and then—preserving little more than the eyes—had placed upon it numerous cutouts in cardboard and silver paper, and a Band-Aid, and a pair of large ears, and cardboard glasses, and a pushpin in the chin. Pencil squiggles served for hair. "It was Rivers's conceit that Norman Mailer wears a false face," Grunwald said. "That is, he saw Mailer's face as a mask with Mailer's own eyes in it." As you stare at Rivers's Mailer, the mask indeed seems to become the face, the face the mask—with eyes at the bottom of cardboard wells. "It seems quite lifelike," I muttered. "One almost expects it to speak."

I looked around the room from cover to cover, NR.

Spiro Agnew. Papier-mâché sculpture by Paul Davis. NR'd because it looked too much like Lyndon Johnson.

Jean-Paul Sartre. By Ben Shahn. Sartre in profile, with sheaves of manuscripts under his arm—*Les Mots*, *La Nausée*, *Saint Genet*. A background of mottled pastels. How could the magazine have rejected that?

It hadn't, Grunwald said. Cover stories on such people had often been swept aside by unexpected developments in the news or lost in a fruitless quest for "the right moment." And, of course, one never knew when a writer might implode. In Sartre's case, the idea for the story had kicked around for years, but the magazine's book-review staff had never pulled itself together enough to produce a story. Of Ben Shahn's work for *Time*, only the Sartre had not run. Shahn had done cover portraits of Lenin, Alec Guinness, Sargent Shriver, Johann Sebastian Bach, Martin Luther King Jr. When Shahn came into the office, he would sit and chatter with Rosemary Frank, the cover researcher, and he would tell her about the Depression days, when he had been a painter for the W.P.A.

W. H. Auden. An oil by René Bouché. A study in wrinkles,

a splendid face. The accompanying story had been written while Otto Fuerbringer, Grunwald's predecessor as managing editor, was away on vacation. Apparently, Otto didn't like Auden, Grunwald said, and Otto came back too soon.

Marilyn Monroe, by Aaron Bohrod. In a pale sky among wisps of cirrus, she stood in an oval picture frame, wearing a string-strap top with a scoop neck. It seemed demure by contemporary lights, an attractive and flattering portrait. One could hardly imagine a better treatment of Monroe. In 1956, Roy Alexander, Fuerbringer's predecessor, had killed it because it was too sexy.

Claes Oldenburg. Self-portrait, on graph paper. His tongue hanging out. An ice bag on his head. "The news, alas, knocked it off the cover," Grunwald said. "The story on Oldenburg ran without the picture."

Time had once planned a cover story on the Establishment, and now here was all that was left of the idea—a painting by Edward Sorel of a turreted, moated medieval castle being defended by substantial, solid-looking University Club types against a horde of scruffy creatures who were carrying a battering ram. On the front end of the battering ram was the severed head of Spiro Agnew. The castle was full of Bundys, Galbraiths, Gardners, McCloys, Achesons, Schlesingers, Oakeses, and Rockefellers, with William F. Buckley Jr., in the form of a flying dragon, hovering in the air above. "It was a better idea than story," Grunwald said, ruefully recalling the wreckage. "The story never worked. We could never quite figure out whether or not we were part of the Establishment, and, if so, how to deal with ourselves."

Grunwald picked up a color transparency that showed a sheaf of wheat, a tragic mask, and the tree of knowledge of good and evil, with the apple partly eaten, so that it looked like a skull, all of which had been created by Salvatore Purpura, a baker, in his bakery, on 111th Street, in Corona, Queens. Purpura had been commissioned to do a *Time* cover on the subject of hunger, and bread was the medium. Purpura was asked at the time what sort of bread he would use, and he said, "Italian bread that you can a-eat." The story was dropped. NR, and a pity, too. Purpura might have become the only baker who had ever baked a cover of *Time*.

Russell Baker, of the *Times*, once came very close to being on *Time*'s cover—close enough to wind up in the NR bin, too, and there he was, in a creation by Herblock, who had used a photograph of Baker's face affixed to a drawing of Baker's body astride a flying newspaper airplane. All through the sky around him were fat-cat senators, congressmen, generals, diplomats. One man's shirtfront was literally exploding. Each of these figures had a toy-balloon valve in his back. Grunwald sighed. "Baker is still writing," he said. "Maybe one day . . . Who knows?"

Norman Laliberte, a designer who uses fabrics and textured materials, had done a handsome tapestry of the Good Samaritan for *Time*'s cover, a grace to the Christmas season, but the tapestry was here in the NR collection, because it had lost out to a stained-glass window, the work of another artist. Grunwald explained that in recent years he had found it expedient to commission more than one artist per cover. Two was now the standard number—two artists competing. Sometimes three. As many as seven artists had been commissioned to do finished paintings for one subject and one issue. The magazine had once depended on a handful of proved regulars, Grunwald said—people like Chaliapin and Boris Artzybasheff. And when

Fuerbringer came along, his predilection had been to commission artists of international celebrity. Grunwald thought some of that had been "a little square." He and his art directors wanted *Time* covers to be "more modern and postery," and they wanted to reach out more for artists who were "unknown." That was risky, so you commissioned several at once. Moreover, if something was not quite right in a picture and it was late getting to the printer, the cost of the delay could run into tens of thousands of dollars. Artists came cheaper. The magazine pays two thousand dollars for a cover painting (more under special circumstances). For a mere six thousand dollars, Grunwald could have three covers among which to choose, thus reducing the possibility of wasting sums much larger.

Artists don't think well of the system. As one has put it, "half my heart isn't in the work." But Grunwald sees no other way in which he can afford to be as experimental as he wants to be—afford, for example, to ask a Gerald Scarfe or a Frank Gallo, or, for that matter, almost anyone else, to try a *Time* cover of Richard Nixon. Nixon, as a face, was by far the most difficult subject that had ever come along. Notwithstanding what might be said in its interior pages, the magazine preferred not to be cruel on the cover. Yet it was difficult not to be. The face—well, the face was just an awkward problem technically. What else could one say? And, to make matters worse, Nixon had appeared on the cover of *Time* more than anyone else ever.

Here, then, was Frank Gallo's Nixon—cast in epoxy resin—looking like the Carnauba Man done in used jaundice. Gallo had sculptured Raquel Welch for *Time* in the same materials. His Raquel figure had been more than life-size, and he had bought an airplane seat for her on his way east to *Time* from his home in Illinois. For his Nixon, he might have bought space in the hold. "It is so ugly we felt we couldn't run it," Grunwald said. "He looks like an embalmed corpse."

And here was the Nixon of Gerald Scarfe, the British cartoonist and papier-mâché sculptor, who had once done the Beatles for *Time*, and had now done what appeared to be an oversize duckbill platypus in papier-mâché. NR.

Grunwald led the way into a room that was overwhelmingly filled with leftover Nixons. During the past year, he said, there was always at least one artist at work on a new try at Nixon. Here now were dozens of them, lining the walls, standing on tables—everywhere you looked, an unused Nixon. Nixon. Nixon. Nixon. Nixon. Nixon. Nixon. Nixon. Nixon. Nixon. Nixon. Nixon. Nixon. Nixon. Nixonixonixonixonixonixon. NR. Not running.

IN THE LONG DRY VALLEYS of eastern Nevada, where rainshadow rain falls in desert rations and the silence is so deep it rings, water has been in storage for about ten thousand years. These are the waterlogged basins, as they are known to science—the saturated valleys—but if you were to look out upon them, that description is the last that would come to your mind. You would, in a glance, take in a million acres with nothing taller than the bunchgrass, the buffalo grass, the shad scale, the white and the black sage in tawny, desiccated boulevards between the high ranges. A daisy-wheel windmill, a cluster of cottonwoods—tens of miles apart—speak of settlement in some of the most austere and beautiful landscape between the oceans. It is a country held together by its concealed water, without which it would become exposed bedrock and dust. To the sub-surface, the amount of fresh supply is essentially zero. What is down there is fossil water, resulting from a time when the climate was utterly different from the climate now, a time when alpine and continental ice to the north, east, and west caused so much rain that the Great Basin of Utah and Nevada held two freshwater lakes about the size of Lake Michigan and Lake Erie. Remains of that Pleistocene rainfall rest beneath the saturated valleys, prevent them from looking like Irq al-Subay, and emerge in small, sustaining quantities as spring creeks and seeps.

Las Vegas wants the water. Las Vegas is in Clark County, in southernmost Nevada, hundreds of miles from the saturated valleys. Distance is not a deterrent when you have the money. In Nevada, you can buy groundwater and, within the law, transport it from one basin to another, provided that the transfer does not impinge upon existing rights and is in the public interest. The public is in Las Vegas—marinopolis of pools and fountains. Las Vegas has less rain than some places in the Sahara, yet its areal population is more than two million. Around Las Vegas, well casings stand in the air like contemporary sculpture, and so much water has been mined from below that the surface of the earth has subsided six feet. While new wells are no longer permissible, Las Vegas desperately needs water for its lakes. They are not glacial lakes. If you want a lake in Las Vegas, you dig a hole and pour water into it. One subdivision has eight lakes. Las Vegas has twenty-two golf courses, at sixteen hundred gallons a divot. Green lawn runs down the median of the Strip. Here is the Wet'n'Wild park, there the M-G-M water rides. Outside the Mirage, a stratovolcano is in a state of perpetual eruption. It erupts water.

Las Vegas wants to drill the saturated valleys, remove the

fossil water to a central place, and then pump it on to the south, in much the way that habitants in Quebec collect maple sap in tubes. Mountain sheep, antelope, deer, coyotes, eagles, badgers, bobcats will forever disappear as permanent springs go permanently dry. Las Vegas blandly claims that the resource is renewable, that Las Vegas will not be mining Nevada's Pleistocene water. All they want to pump up is—annually—the equivalent of a one-acre pond eight hundred and sixty thousand feet deep.

POOLS AND POOLS AND POOLS of chocolate—fifty-thousand-pound, ninety-thousand-pound, Olympic-length pools of chocolate—in the conching rooms in the chocolate factory in Hershey, Pennsylvania. Big, aromatic rooms. Chocolate, as far as the eye can see. Viscous, undulating, lukewarm chocolate, viscidized, undulated by the slurping friction of granite rollers rolling through the chocolate over crenellated granite beds at the bottoms of the pools. The chocolate moves. It stands up in brown creamy dunes. Chocolate eddies. Chocolate currents. Gulfs of chocolate. Chocolate deeps. Mares' tails on the deeps. The world record for the fifty-yard free-style would be two hours and ten minutes.

Slip a little spatula in there and see how it tastes. Waxy? Claggy? Gritty? Mild? Taste it soft. That is the way to get the flavor. Conching—granite on granite, deep in the chocolate—ordinarily continues for seventy-two hours, but if Bill Wagner thinks the flavor is not right, he will conch for hours extra, or even an extra day. Milky? Coarse? Astringent? Caramely? For forty-five years, Bill Wagner has been tasting the chocolate. His taste buds magnified a hundred times would probably look like Hershey's kisses. He is aging now, and is bent slightly forward—a slender man, with gray hair and some white hair. His eyeglasses have metal rims and dark plastic brows. He wears thin white socks and brown shoes, black trousers, a white shirt with the company's name on it in modest letters. Everyone wears a hat near the chocolate. Most are white paper caps. Wagner's hat is dapper, white, visored: a chocolate-making supervisor's linen hat.

A man in a paper hat comes up and asks Wagner, "Are we still running tests on that kiss paste?"

"Yes. You keep testing."

Wagner began in cocoa, in 1924. The dust was too much for him. After a few weeks, he transferred to conching. He has been conching ever since, working out the taste and texture. Conching is the alchemy of the art, the transmutation of brown paste into liquid Hershey bars. Harsh? Smooth? Fine? Bland? There are viscosimeters and other scientific instruments to aid the pursuit of uniformity, but the ultimate instrument is Wagner. "You do it by feel, and by taste," he says. "You taste for flavor and for fineness—whether it's gritty. There's one area of your tongue you're more confident in than others. I use the front end of my tongue and the roof of my mouth." He once ate some Nestlé's; he can't remember when. He lays some chocolate on the tip of his tongue and presses it upward. The statement that sends ninety thousand pounds on its way to be eaten is always the same. Wagner's buds blossom, and he says, "That's Hershey's."

Milton Hershey's native town was originally called Derry Church, and it was surrounded, as it still is, by rolling milkland. Hershey could not have been born in a better place, for milk is twenty per cent of milk chocolate. Bill Wagner grew up on a farm just south of Derry Church. "It was a rented farm. We didn't own a farm until 1915. I lived on the farm through the Second World War. I now live in town." Wagner's father, just after 1900, had helped Milton Hershey excavate the limestone bedrock under Derry Church to establish the foundations of the chocolate plant. Derry Church is Hershey now, and its main street, Chocolate Avenue, has streetlamps shaped like Hershey's kisses—tinfoil, tassel, and all. The heart of town is the corner of Chocolate and Cocoa. Other streets (Lagos, Accra, Para) are named for the places the beans come from, arriving in quotidian trains full of beans that are roasted and, in studied ratios, mixed together—base beans, flavor beans, African beans, American beans—and crushed by granite millstones arranged in cascading tiers, from which flow falls of dark cordovan liquor. This thick chocolate liquor is squeezed mechanically in huge cylindrical accordion compressors. Clear cocoa butter rains down out of the compressors. When the butter has drained off, the compressors open, and out fall dry brown disks the size of manhole covers. The disks are broken into powder. The powder is put into cans and sold. It is Hershey's Cocoa—straight out of the jungle and off to the supermarket, pure as the purest sunflower seed in a whole-earth boutique.

Concentrate fresh milk and make a paste with sugar. To two parts natural chocolate liquor add one part milk-and-sugar paste and one part pure cocoa butter. Conch for three days and three nights. That, more or less, is the recipe for a Hershey bar. (Baking chocolate consists of nothing but pure chocolate liquor allowed to stand and harden in molds. White chocolate is not really chocolate. It is made from milk, sugar, and cocoa butter, but without cocoa.) In the conching rooms, big American flags hang from beams above the chocolate. "Touch this," Bill Wagner says. The cast-iron walls that hold in the chocolate are a hundred and thirty degrees Fahrenheit. "We have no heat under this. It's only created heat—created by the friction that the granite rollers produce."

"What if the rollers stop?"

"The chocolate will freeze."

When that happens, the result is a brown ice cap, a chocolate-coated Nome. Sometimes fittings break or a worker forgets to shut off a valve and thousands of pounds of chocolate spill over, spread out, and solidify on the floor. Workers have to dig their way out, with adzes, crowbars, shovels, and picks.

"The trend today is people want to push buttons," Wagner says. "They'll try to find ways to shortcut. It's a continual struggle to get people to do their share. There's no shortcut to making Hershey's. There have been times when I wished I'd stayed on the farm." Every day, he works from six in the morning until four-thirty in the afternoon, so he can cover parts of all shifts. He walks to work in twelve minutes from his home, on Para Avenue. "Para is a bean, I think. It's a bean or a country, I'm not sure which. We have another street called Ceylon. That's not a bean. It's a country." In the conching rooms, Wagner can see subtleties of hue that escape the untrained eye; he can tell where the kiss paste is, and the semisweet, and the chocolate chips, and the bar milk chocolate. Kiss paste has to be a little more dense, so the kisses will sit up. Wagner has grandchildren in Hershey, Colebrook, and Mechanicsburg. When he goes to see them, he slips them kisses.

Within the connoisseurship, there are dearer chocolates, and, God knows, inferior ones, but undeniably there is no chocolate flavor quite like that of a Hershey bar. No one in Hershey can, or will, say exactly why. There is voodoo in the blending of beans, and even more voodoo in the making of the milk-and-sugar paste. There is magic in Bill Wagner when he decides that a batch is done. All this, however, does not seem to add up to a satisfactory explanation of the uniqueness of the product. Mystery lingers on. Notice, though, in the conching rooms, what is happening to the granite rollers rolling under the chocolate on the granite beds. Slowly, geologically, the granite is eroding. The granite beds last about thirty years. The granite rollers go somewhat sooner than that. Rolling back and forth, back and forth, they become flat on one side. Over the days, months, years, this wearing down of the granite is uniform, steady, consistent, a little at a time. There seems to be an ingredient that is not listed on the label. Infinitesimal granitic particles have nowhere to go but into the chocolate. A Hershey bar is part granite.

Ask management where the granite comes from. The official answer is "New England."

"Where in New England?"

"New England. That is all we are saying. Nestlé's won't say anything about anything. Mars is the same way. So we don't say anything, either."

AT VASSAR COLLEGE, a few decades ago, I read to a gymful of people some passages from books I had written, and then received questions from the audience. The first person said, "Of all the educational institutions you went to when you were younger, which one had the greatest influence on the work you do now?" The question stopped me for a moment because I had previously thought about the topic only in terms of individual teachers and never in terms of institutions. Across my mind flashed the names of a public-school system K through 12, a New England private school (13), and two universities—one in the United States, one abroad—and in a split second I blurted out, "The children's camp I went to when I was six years old."

The response drew general laughter, but, funny or not, it was the simple truth. The camp, called Keewaydin, was at the north end of Lake Dunmore, about eight miles from Middlebury, Vermont. It was a canoeing camp, but in addition to ribs, planking, quarter-thwarts, and open gunwales you learned to identify rocks, ferns, and trees. You played tennis. You backpacked in the Green Mountains on the Long Trail. If I were to make a list of all the varied subjects that have come up in my articles and books, adding a check mark beside interests derived from Keewaydin, most of the entries would be checked. I spent all summer every summer at Keewaydin from age six through fifteen, and later was a counsellor there, leading canoe trips and teaching swimming, for three years while I was in college.

The Kicker was the name of the camp newspaper, and its editor was my first editor, a counsellor named Alfred G. Hare, whose surname translated to the Algonquian as Waboos, a nickname that had been with him from childhood and would ultimately stay with him through his many years as Keewaydin's director. Waboos was a great editor. He laughed in the right places, cut nothing, and let you read your pieces aloud at campfires.

When I first arrived at Keewaydin as a child (my father was the camp's physician), the name Eisner was all over the place—on silver trophies and on the year-by-year boards in the dining hall that listed things like Best Swimmer, Best Athlete, Best Singles Canoe. Michael Eisner was not one of those Eisners.

When I first arrived at Keewaydin, he was still pushing zero. He had five years to wait before he was born. His father, Lester, was among the storied Eisners, and so were assorted uncles and cousins. Over time, multiple Eisners would follow. In 1949, when Lester Eisner brought Michael to the camp to see if he would like to enroll there, I was in the first of my three years as a counsellor in the oldest of the four age groups into which the camp was divided. In the two summers that followed (the last ones for me), he was in the youngest group and I didn't know him from Mickey Mouse. I was aware only that another Eisner had come to Keewaydin.

Summer camps have varying specialties and levels of instruction. They differ considerably in character and mission. No one description, positive or negative, can come near fitting all of them or even very many. Keewaydin was not a great experience for just anybody. My beloved publisher—Roger W. Straus Jr., founder of Farrar, Straus and Giroux—went to Keewaydin when he was thirteen years old and hated every minute of it. That amounts to about eighty thousand minutes. Over the years, he has spent at least a hundred thousand minutes making fun of me for loving Keewaydin. The probable cause is Keewaydin's educational rigor. Gently but firmly, you were led into a range of activity that left you, at the end of the summer, with enhanced physical skills and knowledge of the natural world. You wanted to go back, and back. Mike Eisner went back in 2000 (hardly for the first or last time). He was fifty-eight. Keewaydin was celebrating the career of its eighty-five-year-old emeritus director. Three people spoke at a Saturday-night campfire. Each was introduced only by name, with no mention of any business or profession or affiliation, just, in turn, Peter Hare, Russ Mac-Donald, Mike Eisner. In his blue jeans and ball cap, walking around the flames with his arms waving, Eisner told three hundred pre-teen and early-teen-aged kids escalating stories of his own days at Keewaydin. They listened closely and laughed often. Few, if any, knew who else he was.

[He was the chairman and C.E.O. of Hollywood's Walt Disney Company.]

A PROFESSIONAL WRITER, by definition, is a person clothed in self-denial who each and almost every day will plead with eloquent lamentation that he has a brutal burden on his mind and soul, will summon deep reserves of "discipline" as seriatim antidotes to any domestic chore, and, drawing the long sad face of the pale poet, will rise above his dread of his dreaded working chamber, excuse himself from the idle crowd, go into his writing sanctum, shut the door, shoot the bolt, and in lonely sacrifice turn on the Mets game.

OVER A LONG SYNTHETIC BRUNCH at 521 West Fifty-seventh Street, Dr. Simpey Kuramoto, a microbiologist and food technologist, remarked that he had just about reached the end of his patience with people who seem to believe that nature cannot be artificially reproduced. "It gets you right here," he said. "The consumer thinks anything artificial is bad. The consumer says, 'Don't monkey with Mother Nature.' The consumer has been brainwashed. How do you like your soup?"

In color, texture, body, and flavor, it was not just tomato soup—it was extremely good tomato soup. And yet it was utterly untomatoed, completely artificial.

Even his daughter had been brainwashed, Dr. Kuramoto went on to say. And that had got him most of all, right there. His daughter had "learned" in school that natural vitamins are better than artificial vitamins. Absurd! All natural edibles are made up of chemicals and all artificial edibles are made up of chemicals. The molecules are the same. In good conscience, any health-food store could go totally artificial if it wanted to. How about that cheese?

The "cheese" tasted like Parmesan and had the same nubbly appearance. It had never been closer to Parma than West Fifty-seventh Street, and it contained no cheese.

A synthetic food could actually be an improvement on its natural counterpart, Dr. Kuramoto said. There was, for example, "a great opportunity" for improvement of the lemon. He just could not understand why people went on clinging to the myth of the superiority of nature. If anything, synthetic products were better than natural ones, because natural foods contained, in addition to their basic components, all sorts of little things that should be fed only to laboratory mice. Modern synthetic-food technology, while imitating the flavors of traditional foods with an exactitude not possible until recent times, was also "eliminating the contaminants from the natural product."

The company Dr. Kuramoto works for is called International Flavors & Fragrances. It is traded on the big board and tries to keep everything else about its activities if not secret at least discreet, for its principal business is the ghosting of the "inventions" of its clients. When a major soap maker or confectioner or soft-drink bottler or world-class cosmetic house "creates" a new and exotic fragrance or flavor, the odds are good that the new creation was in fact developed in a laboratory on West Fifty-seventh Street. I.F.F. likes to call itself "a hidden supplier."

Given appropriate incentive, the company will attempt to reproduce any taste or aroma known on the earth. Once, during a famine in India, a mountain of butter was rushed over from the United States to help save lives, but the Indians were suspicious of the butter's unfamiliar flavor and would not touch it. I.F.F. was consulted, and its flavor-and-aroma chemists decided to reproduce the taste and scent of Indian ghee, which, in loose definition, is rancid-smelling water-buffalo butter. Soon, artificial essence of ghee was flown to India and sprayed on the American cow butter, ton after ton of which quickly went down the Indian gullet.

A restaurateur in California once came to I.F.F. with the complaint that his restaurant did not smell particularly enticing, because it lacked, in this age of microwaves, suffusive kitchen aromas. I.F.F. responded with a synthetic scent of baked ham, in aerosol cans, and, complementarily, a spray of chemically fabricated Dutch apple.

A marine museum in Florida, although situated close to the sea, felt that its interior lacked the inspiring smell of brine, kelp, and decaying porgies that is known as "salt air." I.F.F. perfumers synthesized the smell and put it into cans labelled "The Ocean."

Certain new and fast-growing rices, agronomically miraculous, were in some instances ignored by peoples of Southeast Asia because the taste was different from the taste of their old, slow-growing rice. I.F.F. broke down the flavor of the old rice, analyzed it, synthesized it, and sent the synthetic flavor off to be mixed with the new kind of rice, making its taste acceptable.

Such feats are assisted by technological devices like the gas-liquid chromatograph and an instrument that determines nuclear-magnetic resonances. Dr. Kuramoto, who is the director of technical support of I.F.F.'s United States Flavor Division, calls these devices, agglomerately, "the machine." In various combinations, ground-up foods or the smokes and vapors from cooking can be sent through the machine, which "blips out peaks" on a small screen. Each peak represents a pure chemical. Analysis and the art of synthetic combination then begin.

Naturally, our own brunch—in I.F.F.'s Flavor Conference Room—had begun with synthetic orange juice. Dr. Kuramoto and his staff had been grinding up oranges and running them through the machine in an attempt to create artificially what the makers of frozen concentrates have never so much as approached with their wholly natural components: the taste of fresh orange juice. He was full of cautionary prefaces, to the effect that the juice was still developmental. "We still have things to learn," he said. "We can't reproduce—yet—the flavor of a freshly squeezed Valencia. It is frustrating. If we can send a man to the moon and back, my God, we can re-create an orange." Joan Koesterer, a flavor chemist in a white coat, handed me a cup of orange fluid. I gave it a shake to bring out the nose. Dr. Kuramoto looked expectant. His sleeves were rolled up. He seemed on the verge of getting up and going to feed the machine another Valencia. A Ph.D. from the University of Minnesota, he had behind him a long stint at General Mills, where he had helped develop meat "analogues" (ham, chicken, bacon—

fabricated from machine-processed soybeans), and now he was going to capture citrus alive or know why not.

I upended my cup and confessed to Dr. Kuramoto that I had once written fifty thousand words about orange juice as a result of a compulsive orange-juice binge that went on for several months and thousands of miles of questing the subtropics. Nowhere had I tasted anything that came nearly as close to the flavor of freshly squeezed orange juice as the fluid there in his lab. Moments before, it had been a powdered mixture of laboratory chemicals.

With the soup course, we drank a form of "strawberry yogurt" that was a laboratory try not only to improve the flavor of a natural strawberry but also to invent a thinned (and artificial) yogurt. Together, they might become a novel beverage. It was a little too novel for me. We then had some terrific devilled ham that consisted wholly of textured soy protein, flavored with chemicals. We ate, as well, tuna and hamburgers that had been doubled in volume with I.F.F.-flavored soya, and washed them down with some "Coca-Cola" that might have caused a riot in Atlanta. "You have heard of the 'secret formula' of Coca-Cola and how it is kept locked away and is known only to a few people?" Dr. Kuramoto said. "Well, have a drink of this."

I drank the "Coke." It was flavor plagiarism, all right—I couldn't tell it from the real thing. Dr. Kuramoto said, "That one was not particularly difficult. We could as easily do Pepsi, too."

Dessert included a so-so milk chocolate, an excellent artificial-chocolate ice milk, and a clear beverage, brown and carbonated, that had the precise aroma of a richly concocted chocolate malted milk but looked like root beer. It had a fine, accurate chocolate-malt taste and contained neither chocolate nor malt. It was, Dr. Kuramoto explained, I.F.F.'s tilt at the windmill of chocolate soda pop—one of the few fields of potentiality in which chocolate has never caught on.

I left Dr. Kuramoto and went off to the office of Van Vechten Sayre, the firm's public-relations expert, who had collected some seventeen artificial fragrances intended to put a finishing sniff to the day. "What's that?" he said, spraying baked ham in my face. "And that?"

"Dutch apple."

"That?"

"The ocean."

"That?"

"Norway spruce, balsam fir."

The spruce-balsam smell had been made for the American Museum of Natural History, where—in the Hall of the North American Forests—machines that contain timing devices press down periodically on the valves of aerosol cans full of instant wilderness. Other I.F.F. cans spray hay into the Hall of South Asiatic Mammals, grass into the Hall of Man in Africa, and a scent called South Pacific (a combination of frangipani and ocean air) into the Margaret Mead wing (Hall of Pacific Peoples). Sayre sprayed me with these things, too. I liked the hay and the grass, but South Pacific was overpowering, and would have overpowered Sadie Thompson.

Sayre brought out a collection of small bottles and a packet of perfumers' blotters, long and thin, and he dipped a blotter into a bottle, then waved it in the air. Eggnog. Another blotter: Mince pie. Another: Apple.

Caramel. Tea. Fresh paint. Cedar. Butter pecan. Irish coffee. Each was as distinct as it was synthetic.

"What's this?" he said now.

"Don't know," I said. "It smells like an entire floral shop."

"It *is* a floral shop," he said. "Now try this one. Think carefully. Where are you?"

I sniffed, and had an instant reaction—a wild, insane thought—and tried to put it aside. For who would want such a thing? Who would think of it, anyway, and how could chemists conceivably get it into a bottle, even if they did think of it? The lichen was there, though, and the moss, the drip, the dank, the chalky scent of the stalagmite, the faint essence of slumbering bear.

"Cave!" I burst out. "A cave!"

He handed me the bottle. The label said "Cave."

BY THE TIME I met David Brower, in 1969, he was more indoors than out. He was only ten years younger than the twentieth century, and he had spent a large part of his life escaping interior scenes by getting himself up into the Sierra and away from confinements of both the natural and the figurative kind. He was shy, and that spurred him, too, to get away. He came to know the mountain country in such detail that it was said of him that he would know exactly where he was if, magically, a hand were to set him down anywhere at all from Sequoia National Forest to the Feather River. He took up technical climbing, and became the first person to touch thirty-seven Sierran peaks. By his account, he would have liked to choose one and stay there.

When incursions in various forms threatened his Sierra,

though, he had to come down and fight. He fought in rooms, theatres, halls, and chambers, and in a way that Homer would best understand. His voyages through the Sierra Club and Friends of the Earth and Earth Island Institute and other loci for defenders of his faith were punctuated with mutiny, fratricide, and triumph. He was feisty, heaven knew. And arrogant, possibly. And relentless, certainly. And above all, effective—for he began his mission when ecology connoted the root-and-shoot relationships of communal plants, and he, as much or more than anyone in the mid-century, expanded its reach and inherent power until it became the environmental movement. Others in time would learn more than he knew and advance the argument in a stabilizing way, but they would always be following him.

I spent a year with him, going from halls to chambers and from city to city, East and West. Blessedly, it was a year of rivers and redwoods and mountains, too. Among scenes and anecdotes that are now reassembling and crowding the mind, one minor and peripheral moment somehow lingers at the center. We were crossing the Mojave Desert. Not on foot. And after an hour or two of the Mojave, Dave Brower remarked that in the give and take of environmental politics—in the long wrestle with opposing forces lined up on countless vectors—he would be willing, if necessary, in the name of diplomacy and compromise, to surrender the Mojave.

I asked him if he would enumerate terrains of his choosing that might be put in the same category. His wife—his gyroscope, Anne—sitting beside him seemed to smile. His son Ken, hitherto somnolent in the back seat, sat up, and said, "It's going to be a short list!"

It was something shorter than that, for Brower looked around a little more at the Mojave, and changed his mind.

A LITTLE BOY is going to come to New York someday, disappear, then eventually return to his hometown as a middle-aged man. When his mother says, "Where were you all this time?," he will tell her: "In the line at the Radio City Music Hall." He may even introduce her to the girl he met near the end of the queue, courted between Fifth Avenue and Rockefeller Plaza, and married at Sixth and Fiftieth.

Sometimes three-quarters of a mile long, forming as early as six-thirty A.M., doubling and redoubling upon itself through a maze of sawhorses set up by New York police, the line of people waiting to get into the Music Hall is one of the phenomena of modern show business. Extra long in the tourist summer (seventy per cent out-of-towners), it is something to see in winter as well, knee-deep in slush and ready for Donner Pass. The Music Hall somehow signifies to the rest of the nation the epicenter of Manhattan. Most of the standees agree with the one who said he was there because "everybody down home just knows about it," and the chap six laps behind him who said, "It's unavoidable, like the Grand Canyon."

When they finally get inside, audiences see a three-hour program—roughly two-thirds movie and one-third stage show—that is anything but just another overpromoted metropolitan swindle. The customers are paying for spectacorn, and the Music Hall is equipped to give it to them. The organ can sound like everything from a Chinese gong to a glockenspiel, and vibrates so profoundly that it probably shows up on seismographs. The fixed lighting system is one of the most advanced in the world, making possible spectacular fireworks and the fondly re-membered burning of Nome. Once every three hours, the Alaskan town collapsed onstage in a cold conflagration of light, silk, and air. Fountain displays have slopped more than a hundred and fifty tons of water onto the stage per day. Niagara Falls once poured out of the wings. A full-size train chugged uphill. One show used a helicopter, another a four-engine bomber, and a third shot satellites into the flies. Chariots have been drawn by live horses galloping on treadmills. Ships have been torpedoed and sunk, descending via the huge, tripartite stage elevator. The Christmas show always features a crèche program, and at Easter time the stage turns into a cathedral, and the women of the corps de ballet turn into nuns, forming a vast human cross, holding lilies in their hands.

WHEN NEIL SIMON was newly married, he and his wife, Joan, moved into an apartment in a brownstone on East Tenth Street in Manhattan. It was four flights up, plus the additional steps of the front stoop. When deliverymen arrived with the furniture, they collapsed on it and sat there for a quarter of an hour with their mouths open and only the whites of their eyes showing. One piece of furniture was a large single bed. In the Simons' bedroom it reached from wall to wall. To get to the closet, they had to walk over the bed. It might have seemed more sensible to sleep in the living room, but a skylight there had a considerable hole in it, and, in winter, snow frequently came pouring through.

All this sounds more like the start of a successful theatrical comedy than a successful marriage, but it turned out to be both. The marriage has been running ten years. Neil Simon's comedy *Barefoot in the Park* may run that long, too. With Robert Redford as a rough facsimile of himself and Elizabeth Ashley as his spritely wife, the play precisely duplicates the events, rents, and blizzards of the Simons' golden past, with delivery-men reeling into view like sherpas out of shape, and the young couple fighting the plausible battles of youth:

He: Let's discuss it.

She: Not with you in the room.

RICHARD HUBER IS THE DEAN of the School of General Studies at Hunter College. He is a leathery tennis competitor, toughest near the finish, calling his opponents "victims." We play each other at least a dozen times a year. Huber is the author of, among other books, *The American Idea of Success*, which comes wrapped in a dust jacket that shows an apple pie in a blue sky. He may write about Norman Vincent Peale and Dale Carnegie, but Huber himself was invented by Stephen Potter, the author of *The Theory and Practice of Gamesmanship*. In the middle of matches, Huber offers you lessons. He is a master of the premature congratulation. Once, after I beat him in the first set, he politely excused himself, went off and took a shower. It was all his after he came back.

In the great pyramid of tennis players—hundreds of thousands of tennis players—everyone up to the ninety-ninth percentile is a permanent and irreparable hack. Not everyone accepts this as axiomatic, for who in the world has never hit a crisp winning backhand down the line, a Wagnerian fore-hand beyond return, a drop volley that screws itself into the ground? My friend Jerry Goodman, for example, has made all these shots, and in his subconscious something has been tell-ing him that he should be able to string them together like beads. As "Adam Smith," he has, after all, written two con-secutive best sellers. So why not two consecutive backhands? We have been playing each other for many years, and I have studied the development of his game. He has a quick eye and a fair mind, and he never calls a ball out until, coming toward him, it has crossed the net and begun its descent toward the ground.

Jim Miller's early flaws were that he never bent his knees, always hit off his back foot, and chopped straight down on his return of serve. He has been proed over by the very best. Don Budge tried to teach him. So did Pancho Segura, Luis Ayala, Alex Olmedo. To get up the money to pay for their instruc-tions, Miller wrote, among other things, *Days of Wine and Roses*. We play at the Mercer County Tennis Center, on the edge of Trenton, where he shows up with a bag of Band-Aids, salt pills, moleskin, rosin spray, headbands, wristbands, and various braces for his principal joints. Miller hasn't had an in-hibition in thirty years. Jokes, insults, and fragments of song come flying across the net from him in a direction somewhat firmer than the direction of his shots, which are hit stiff-kneed off his back foot and are frequently chopped straight down.

Bill Dwyer is my doubles partner in minor regional tour-naments, and he says that he has carried me through more matches than he can remember. That may be. Dwyer also takes pride in saying that, many years ago, he worked his way through

college. That may be, too—but he certainly didn't do it hustling tennis players. Dwyer knows, though, the seminal secret of hackery: you do what you can do and never what you can't do—you never try to overcome your flaws. If you have a net game and no ground strokes, you rush the net headlong no matter what the books say, what surface you are playing on, or where the last shot happened to go.

TENNIS ROSTER OF THE SEVENTIES for a charity event at Forest Hills:

ASHE. . . . Mind wanders. Does crossword puzzles in his head while hitting backhands down the line.

DELL. . . . Dell and Laver of an age. Dell defeated Laver once, in same week began to shave. Good underspin lob. Excellent bouncing overhead. Weakness: returning balls that come back. A lawyer. A major impresario in modern anarchic tennis. He manages the fiscal fates of Ashe, Smith, Roche, Ralston, Riessen, McManus, Pasarell, Lutz, Kodeš, Franulović. Even on a tennis court, he cannot stand to be away from a telephone. Has replaced his navel with a jack.

DRYSDALE. . . . Tall. Elegant. South African. Tough two-handed backhand—looks something like Ted Williams punching out a single. Consistent quarterfinalist. Rarely has a bad loss.

DÜRR. . . . French Algerian, called Frankie. Learned the game in Algiers. She is radiantly unorthodox. Ping-Pong-grip backhand. Quixote forehand. Impressive results. A teacher's nightmare but never a linesman's. Never complains.

GONZALES. . . . Known as Gorgo, diminutive of Gorgonzola. Chronological age: forty-four. Physical age: twenty-six. Grandfather. Recently beat Laver, Smith, and Ashe in consecutive matches in Las Vegas. Awesomely quick for six feet three, moves like a big cat. First won Forest Hills 1948. Southwest Open champion, 1971. Much between.

GORMAN. . . . Seattle. Best ever from Pacific Northwest. Regional hero. Rising. All-court player. Happy, carefree, funny, and subtle. Concentration occasionally splays. Biggest win was in straight sets over Laver at Wimbledon, 1971.

KODEŠ. . . . Law student. Married. Czech. The best since Drobný. French champion 1970, 1971. Described tennis on grass as "a joke," then hit his way into the Forest Hills final. Has faculty for returning bullet serves as fresh bullets.

LAVER. . . . Last year in some ways his worst of recent times (82–18), when his prize money surpassed Nicklaus, the most golden of golfers, by nearly fifty thousand dollars. Grew up on a cattle farm in tropical Australia. Homemade tennis court. Had to wait his turn while his older brothers played. His turn would come. Record unique. Two Grand Slams (only three have ever been made). Four Wimbledons. He is the greatest player the game has so far seen.

LUTZ. . . . Halfback. Loved football so much he decided in 1965 to give up tennis if he did not win National Junior Championship. National Junior champion, 1965.

McKINLEY. . . . Reared in Saint Louis. Educated in Texas. Anointed in England. Enriched in New York. Won Wimbledon 1963, retired straightaway into brokerage business.

NEWCOMBE. . . . Writes with great lucidity about subtle points of tennis, practices what he writes. Grew up in Sydney,

now lives on a ranch in New Braunfels, Texas—an exotic parabola, studded with Wimbledons (three). He is also a doubles player outstanding in all time, having won twice at Forest Hills and five times at Wimbledon (four with Roche).

OKKER. . . . High-strung. Nervous. Known as "The Twitch." Twitched $120,465 off the pro tour last year. Five feet eight, 140 pounds, not much power. He intimidates with speed. He is Dutch. When he was born, his family was in hiding, hunted by Nazis.

PASARELL. . . . Tenacious. Unpredictable. Powerful. Textbook tennis player, picture serve. Tends to get involved in extraordinarily unusual matches. Two examples. Gonzales beat him 22–24, 1–6, 16–14, 6–3, 11–9 at Wimbledon in 1969, second-longest tennis match ever played. Pasarell defeated Santana at Wimbledon in 1967, only time in the history of Wimbledon that a defending champion has been beaten on opening day.

ROSEWALL. . . . Has resided on the highest level of the game for twenty years. No drink. No smoke. Bedtime: sunset. Grew up in Sydney, where his father, a grocer, owned three tennis courts and rented them to augment the family income. Developed strokes so graceful they are the canon of the game. Too small for serve-and-volley bludgeon tennis. Nickname: Muscles.

SMITH. . . . Basketball player. Good jump shot. Fair set shot. Moves well without the ball. Turned to tennis at advanced age (upper teens), five years later was in his first Wimbledon final. Current Forest Hills and Wimbledon champion. Way to beat him is to lift his wallet, which he keeps under umpire's chair.

DURING THE RUN of the Ziegfeld Follies of 1917, a man in his mid-fifties kept reappearing in the audience night after night—always buying two tickets, one for himself, one for his hat—to stare at a blond chorine named Marion Davies. He already had a wife, five sons, a gold mine, seven magazines, ten newspapers, more than a million acres of land—and now he wanted the chorine. Getting her was as easy for William Randolph Hearst as hailing a taxicab. Remarkably, she remained his mistress for thirty-four years.

Hearst made plans to build Marion into the supreme star of American films. Born Marion Cecilia Douras, a daughter of a small-time New York politician, she was still in her teens; her convent education had stopped some years earlier. But Hearst bought a Harlem studio, established his own film company, hired tutors and drama coaches, the best scenarists, set designers, and directors, to help shape his Galatea. For the opening of her film *Cecilia of the Pink Roses*, in 1918, he had the theatre ventilating system loaded with attar of roses, bathing the audience in florid scent. His newspapers, of course, hailed the new star's birth with eight-color superlatives in reviews that ran below eight-column headlines.

Marion stuttered and blinked simultaneously, but that hardly mattered to Hearst, who spent millions on prototype superspectacles—and happily lost money on most of them, always casting Marion as a kind of imperial virgin. Full of fun and laughter, with a clear eye for the absurd, Marion called him Pops, and liked to run her fingers through his sterling-silver

hair. She would have become his wife as well, but Hearst's wife, Millicent, herself a former chorine, steadily denied Hearst his request for a divorce.

When the film capital shifted from New York to Hollywood, Hearst arranged for Metro-Goldwyn-Mayer to pay Marion ten thousand dollars a week in return for her talented services. For Marion, Hearst constructed on the M-G-M lot a fourteen-room, seventy-five-thousand-dollar mansion, calling it the "Bungalow." Good-hearted, free-spending Marion dispensed Hearst's money with a generous hand, quickly becoming the most popular actress at the studio, paying doctor bills for office boys, distributing expensive gifts to grips and electricians, even paying a studio newsboy's tuition at a private school.

Hearst haunted the sets of Davies pictures, giving two dozen orders a minute to hapless directors. After Norma Shearer managed to beat out his protégée for a part, Hearst told his editors from coast to coast never to mention Shearer's name in print. With uncanny foresight, Hearst papers could be counted on for banner headlines such as "MARION DAVIES' GREATEST FILM OPENS TONIGHT."

As film fatales went, Marion was not a complete zero, and non-Hearst critics—including *The New York Times*—now and then gave her a line of modest praise. But her pictures continued to lose money, and, since it had been apparent for some time to both of them that she never would become another Mary Pickford, in 1937 Marion made her last picture. She and Pops more or less settled down to the life of Midas—at their fifty-five-bathroom, three-million-two-hundred-and-fifty-thousand-dollar beach palace in Santa Monica, and the twin-towered thirty-million-dollar Hearst castle at San Simeon.

At the fabled house parties, the aging Hearst persisted in

limiting pre-dinner cocktails to one per person, but Marion Davies and Carole Lombard would remedy that in the ladies' bathroom. After Calvin Coolidge spent a weekend with Hearst, Marion complained, "All they talked about was their g-g-g-goddamned circulation."

Extreme old age had no effect on Hearst's extreme jealousy. As they always had, his eyes followed Marion wherever she moved; her leading men were afraid to enter wholeheartedly into on-camera kisses, since Hearst's newspapers had ruined other men's careers for less cause. When Hearst's own empire was facing ruin in the Depression thirties, Marion loaned Hearst back a million dollars, and won his lifetime gratitude. Still in her forties when Hearst was in his eighties, Marion remained loyal until Hearst died, reading to him, nursing him during the four years between his heart attack and his death, in 1951.

Twenty years earlier on the lot at M-G-M, after answering an interrupting phone call from Pops, she had turned smiling to a friend and stuttered out a line that could someday be her epitaph: "H-h-h-hearst come, H-h-h-hearst served."

DO I REMEMBER when I had my first drink? Absolutely. We were playing football at the corner of Prospect Avenue and Murray Place. I was ten years old. We're talking whiskey. I have no idea what kind. This was pickup, sandlot, no-pads, tackle football on a vacant lot that was owned by Princeton University. We played there often. One day somebody showed up late,

carrying a bottle he had discovered in a building on the college campus.

He was one of us—our age, our pal, our teammate—but he had an advanced sense of the people up the street who were no longer in grade school. The bottle was three-quarters full. The football game went into a long time-out. There was a big tulip poplar at one end of the vacant lot (it is still there, spread above someone's house), and we sat down in a circle under the tree for an experiment in precursive maturity. The sniff. The snort. The dilation of the nose. The glowing briquette in the throat. As the gastroentomologist Ian Frazier has reflected after munching brown-drake mayflies, it was hard to stop at just one. Across fifteen, twenty minutes, I took in several gulps of whatever it was. One thing it wasn't was unpleasant.

What time is it? Omigod, I have a piano lesson with Miss Jackson and I'm already fifteen minutes late.

I got up, mounted my bicycle, and raced for home.

Randomly, we played our football games in various places around the town, one of which was the front lawn of the Institute for Advanced Study. The lawn was framed by a double row of sycamores, whose big unforgiving trunks marked our sidelines. We sometimes had an audience of one. Walking to work from his house on Mercer Street, Albert Einstein, leonine and sockless, would stop for a while to watch the action. He did not cheer. He never said anything. And before long he would move on. But he seemed interested, seemed to understand what he was looking at, even if we did not. He had been in Princeton six or seven years then, and would remain on Mercer Street for the rest of his life. Lots of kids growing up in Princeton at the time had stories to tell about him. He helped some of them with their math homework.

But those were other days and this was a bike sprint up Murray Place to Maple Street under pressured conditions. I skidded into our gravel driveway, jumped off the bicycle, and ran into the living room through the side door. Miss Laverne Jackson was there, long since there, at the piano, looking at sheet music, and pointedly sitting on half of the bench. Running past her, I went out of the living room, up the stairs, and down the hall to a bathroom, where I grabbed a tube of Colgate toothpaste. With both hands around it, I aimed it into my mouth and squeezed. My father was a teetotaler, never touched a drop, and I often heard him sneer about the scent of liquor on people's breath. A ton of Colgate hit the roof of my mouth. Then I squished it so hard that it emerged between my teeth. I spit it out and ran downstairs to my side of the piano bench. Miss Jackson was impassive. She had nothing more to say than Einstein did. She was young and well trained. Her concerts ran from Debussy and Chopin to Beethoven and Bach, but giving lessons was still her livelihood.

I played "Country Gardens." I think I played it well, because it is hard not to. It is the teething ring of pianism.

I was in my fourth year of piano lessons. Miss Jackson had scheduled me to play "Country Gardens" in a public recital.

Mi mi re do do
Ti ti la sol sol
La ti mi fa
La sol fa mi.

In preference to watching my hands on the keyboard, she seemed to be watching me as I did the repeat:

Mi mi re do do
Ti ti la sol sol
La ti mi fa
La sol fa mi.
Dah dah doo dah
Dah dah dah dah doo dah
Dah dum dum
Dah dum
Dum dee dum.

Out of my mouth came a large frosted bubble, dah doo, followed by another large frosted bubble.

WHEN MARTHA, my youngest daughter, was seventeen, her English teacher—Mrs. Thomas—wrote forty-seven vocabulary words on the blackboard and told the class to write a short composition using all forty-seven words: aspersion, audacious, avarice, blanch, blight, brusque, buffeted, caprice, cataclysm, charlatan, collude, concomitantly, condign, contiguous, cynosure, decorum, depreciatory, desultory, diaphanous, dilatory, discursive, dispersion, éclat, effulgence, elucidate, emollient, empyreal, enervated, equivocal, erudite, felicity, fiscal, flaccid, fortuitous, gamut, gazette, gregarious, habitat, haggard, homogeneous, innovative, nectarine, oscillate, procrastinate, progeny, prognosticate, and recalcitrant. Martha handed in five paragraphs—four hundred and fifty-two words in all. One out of ten words in her composition was a word from Mrs. Thomas's blackboard:

It is with great felicity that I begin this profile of my father. He is an interesting man. When I say interesting, I do not mean to be equivocal. There are many adjectives that could elucidate his personality. He is certainly erudite and a kind man. He is at the same time spontaneous and inflexible. One could not call him a charlatan, but one could say he is changeable. There are days when there seems to be no end of cataclysms in his world. On those days he does not show decorum, nor does he blanch at confronting the crises. In fact, he does not allow himself to be buffeted by the caprices of the day. He does not oscillate between audacious and conciliatory behavior. He stands firm.

My father has certain problems about money. It is fortuitous that he is in excellent fiscal shape. His problem is not avarice, but it comes when he is faced with the dispersion of money. In other words, when he has to spend money he first procrastinates and then becomes brusque with any one asking for it. Eventually if the "asker" persists, especially if it is his progeny, he loses his gregarious personality. He appears to be enervated, almost flaccid. He loses any of his normal éclat and his face becomes haggard. When my three sisters and I collude in order to get some additional funds, we run the gamut of all possible means. We are innovative and at the same time we invoke all known ploys. In our habitat, otherwise known as our home, we are a homogeneous foursome. We are never dilatory or desultory; we go directly for the jugular. My father considers us his financial blight. As he becomes discursive, arguing for frugality, we become recalcitrant, arguing for luxury.

It is at this point my father may cast aspersions on the way in which we operate. It is then that we try another method. We become nectarine. Our very tongues act as an emollient to his sternness. We appear as empyreal, and concomitantly he appears as grasping and scroogelike. I can never prognosticate the ending of these encounters, but I can promise there is no effulgence of cash. My father, who writes for a gazette, has an office contiguous with his bedroom. If we come out of that fetid office with a few extra dollars, we consider ourselves fortunate. After we go shopping, I come home with a diaphanous gown. I am the cynosure of our small constellation of females. Could one call this a condign profile of my father? I am afraid I have been depreciatory. We are actually a heterogeneous group that on most occasions gets on quite well together.

EVERYONE KNOWS who Richard Burton is, or at least what he is at the moment. He is the demi-Atlas of this earth, the arm and burgonet of men, the fellow who is living with Elizabeth Taylor. Stevedores admire him. Movie idols envy him. He is a kind of folk hero out of nowhere, with an odd name like Richard instead of Tab, Rock, or Rip, who has out-Tabbed, out-Rocked, and out-Ripped the lot of them. If only he were indeed from nowhere, his dazzle would be unshadowed. But beyond the flaring headlines of the past year, few are aware of who Richard Burton really is, what he has done, and what he is

throwing away by gulping down his past and then smashing the glass.

Not too long ago, Richard Burton was considered one of the half-dozen great actors in the English-speaking world. Other actors equally select—Paul Scofield, Sir Laurence Olivier—recognized this; so did critics like Kenneth Tynan; so did a growing public, aware that Burton was young and that most of his major work was still to be done. He has not done it, and there is more than a slight possibility that he never will. But no one can take from him, at least, the achievements that are already behind him. In Stratford-upon-Avon and the Old Vic, he has delivered some nine or ten major Shakespearean performances. Only four actors in history have played Prince Hamlet more than a hundred times in a single production—Sir Henry Irving, Sir Herbert Beerbohm Tree, Sir John Gielgud, and Richard Burton. Moreover, Burton was the longest-running Hamlet in the history of the Old Vic, where Hamlets were kept in the repertory only as long as the box office remained strong.

Today, his profession views Burton with melancholy. "When the movie career is finished," sighs Gielgud, "he will have lost his romantic years, his vigorous years." His friend and agent, Harvey Orkin, has said roughly, "This is a man who sold out. He's trying to get recognition on a trick. He could have been the greatest actor on this planet." It was Olivier who first warned Burton, "Make up your mind. Do you wish to be a household word or a great actor?" Paul Scofield gauges his language with care: "Richard professionally is the most interesting actor to have emerged since the war. I think his qualities of heroic presence are not seen to their fullest advantage in movies. He appears not to be attracted by the best that there is in

the cinema. As for his future, he should return quietly to the theatre."

Whether Burton ever does return to the theatre—in more than a token way—will be determined by something considerably deeper than the fate of the liaison he has recently formed. Two little gods within his frame are warring—one that builds with sureness and power, and another that impels him, like his late companion and countryman Dylan Thomas, recklessly toward self-destruction.

Either way, he is a man and a half. He has a wild mind with a living education in it. He is bright and perceptive to an alarming degree, a rare and dangerous thing in an actor. He laughs honestly. He lies winningly. He trusts absolutely. He can make anyone laugh. He can talk a person under the table about literature, displaying huge sophistication and no cant. He reads rapidly, but he gives a book its due—a novel like *Anglo-Saxon Attitudes* costs him only two hours, but *Moby-Dick* is worth four days, and Robert Burton's *Anatomy of Melancholy* took him "just over three months." He is a walking concordance to Shakespeare. His mind rings with English verse from all centuries and of all qualities, both great and frivolous. "Edward VII was ill," he will say with a brooding smile, "and the poet laureate—this bloody fool—wrote:

Along the wires the electric message came:
'He is no better, he is much the same.'"

Burton has pale blue-green eyes, finely textured brown hair, and a coarse complexion, which is said to contribute to his enormous appeal to women. But even more, women lose their balance over his look of essential melancholy. His face can light suddenly with a smile, but it always returns to its primal gloom.

He talks to everyone as if they matter. It is his special gift, seldom found in actors, or, for all that, in clergymen. Burton's

secret is simple. Everyone actually does matter to him. He tells more stories than Scheherazade, but between them, he listens. He really wants to hear about one man's children or another's Sunday football match. He can make people feel larger than life. Men appreciate him for it; but women write him letters, chase him around tables, and follow him overseas.

Life with Burton was never quiet. He sleeps five hours, no more, and he has the energy to skip sleep altogether and work steadily the following day. He can sit at a piano all night flogging Welsh songs or playing miscellaneous mood pieces, usually incongruous, while he recites poetry, now mocking the voice of Gielgud, now mimicking Olivier, slipping into the tongue of Richard Burton when he does something that holds particular gravity for him. He doesn't swear like a trooper (he barks at Taylor for her vulgarisms), being too much in love with words to settle for slang.

He says he wants more than anything else to be alone, but his dressing-room door is always open to cronies of all ages and sexes. People not only like him, they come near to worshipping him, often for a good reason. Once, in *Camelot*, a young boy was put into the show green and frightened, and during his first rehearsal with Burton he froze. Burton purposely began to stutter, stumble, and quiver. It was one of his most adroit performances. The boy's nerves receded; his voice coughed into life. He still writes to Burton once a month.

Once, after fluffing the same line repeatedly on a movie set, Burton lowered his head and rammed it into a wall. It is impossible to imagine an English actor doing that, but Burton of course is not English. He is Welsh. In fact, he is so thoroughly, defensively, and patriotically Welsh that it costs him some loss

of perspective. His gallery of great Welshmen includes Louis XIV, Christopher Columbus, and Alexander the Great.

He remembers James Joyce's belief that every man spends his life looking for the place he wants to belong to. "I think I grew up in the place I have dreamed of all my life," he says. It is a village in a valley between high loaves of bald green mountains, split by a small river of rushing white water—called, oddly enough, the Avon—and spanned by a high, narrow stone bridge that was once an aqueduct. Poverty has seldom had a more graceful setting. The village even has a euphonically romantic name—Pontrhydyfen (*pontra de venne*)—and, particularly in Richard Burton's view, it is a kind of Glamorganshire Brigadoon. "When I go home," he says, "as I go around the lip of the mountain, my heart races."

He was born in Pontrhydyfen on the tenth of November, 1925. His father—Richard Jenkins—was a miner with little more to his name than a No. 6 shovel and a massive gift for words. Richard was the twelfth of thirteen children. His mother died when he was not quite two, just after giving birth to Richard's brother Graham. In Taibach, a suburb of the coastal town Port Talbot, at the foot of the Avon, Richard was devotedly raised by his eldest sister, Cecilia. He went to school in Port Talbot, but he spent his weekends in Pontrhydyfen. The town spoke English and the village spoke Welsh; hence Richard was raised bilingual. He was also raised with a powerful sense of belonging to a village where he could not live.

"My father was a self-taught man, demoniacal in debate, agnostic, with a divine gift of the tongue in both languages. He used hyperbole. He was not afraid of the octosyllabic word. He had a sort of maxim—'Never use a short word where a long

one will do.' He was a Welsh Pushkin in conversation. He would go off on jags that would make John Barrymore look sedate. He never knew which son I was. He was fifty when I was born. We called him Daddy Ni, which means 'our father.' He sometimes frightened me. His mind was extraordinarily perverse. No one quite knew what he was going to do next, which can be quite frightening to a child, you know."

Daddy Ni died in 1957, never having seen Richard in a play or movie. He tried once—setting out to see *My Cousin Rachel* when it was playing in a Port Talbot cinema. On the way down the valley, he stopped in seventeen pubs. Finally settled in the theatre, he watched the film begin. One of the first things Richard did on the screen was to pour himself a drink. "That's it," said Daddy Ni, and he was up and off to pub No. 18.

Daddy Ni cared more about education than anything else, even Rugby football, and from Richard's earliest memory Daddy Ni and Richard's brothers Ivor, Tom, Will, and Dai fixed their attention on Richard and said, "You shall go to Oxford." All the brothers save Graham had worked the coal face (Richard himself never worked in the mines), and some of them went on to other positions in local government, the police, and the army. In Richard, however, the family planted its dream of something better beyond the valley. "The idea of a Welsh miner's son going to Oxford University," Richard Burton says, "was ridiculous beyond the realm of possibility."

First, Richard was one of thirty who were admitted to grammar school out of some six hundred applicants. He was also an athlete and, of all things, a gifted soprano who took prizes in the eisteddfod, singing, as his sister put it, as if "he had a bell in every tooth." In a sense, he outgrew his family, being something more than life-size even then. A teacher-writer

named Philip Burton, drama coach and English master at the Port Talbot grammar school, offered him a room in his lodgings. Cecilia and her husband agreed.

Richard describes himself as "mock tough" when he first knew Philip Burton. Burton, for his part, was chiefly impressed, in Richard's first awkward go on a stage, by the boy's "astonishing audience control—he could do anything he wanted with the audience." This is one talent that can only be found, never developed, and since Richard had it, Phil Burton trained him dramatically, put an English polish on his voice without obscuring the Welsh vitality, fed him a reading list of great books, prepared him for his try for Oxford, and directed him in all his early plays. In 1943, Richard officially became Phil Burton's ward, taking his name. Years later, when Richard was told that his father was dead, he asked, "Which one?"

Phil Burton trained Richard with some novel devices. He made him talk on five telephones at once, doing a scene from a play about a busy bank manager who could hold five separate conversations, darting from phone to phone. The exercise was repeated a thousand times to teach the boy coordination and mathematical precision in speaking. Today, Richard understandably hates telephones, but he speaks with fantastic precision. Also, Phil Burton would take Richard to the summit of Mynydd Margam, the last high mountain between Pontrhydyfen and the sea, and have him loft arias from Shakespeare into the wind. As Phil Burton moved farther and farther from the spot on which Richard stood, he kept calling, "Make me hear you. Don't shout, but make me hear you." Ten years later, as Richard would all but whisper, "O! what a rogue and peasant slave am I," every princely syllable went special delivery to the outermost rafters of the Old Vic.

The academic training succeeded as well. Richard was accepted by Exeter College, Oxford. The R.A.F. conveniently provided a scholarship, indenturing him to air service later on. He had to wait two terms before he would actually be *in statu pupillari*, so he answered an ad in Wales's *Western Mail*, placed by the actor Emlyn Williams, seeking a young Welsh actor for a play called *The Druid's Rest*. He got the part and spent five months in the West End, going up to Oxford as a slightly seasoned professional.

It was wartime Oxford, but no war to date has changed the ways of the university, and Burton was soon climbing into the college after late and beery forays. He boasts that he broke the Exeter sconce record, a complicated dining-hall punishment for bad etiquette, in which the offender was forced to drink nearly two pints of beer in thirty seconds or pay for it. He learned to drink without swallowing and could put down a sconce in ten seconds. "So far as I know," he says, "no one has ever whacked that feat."

He was ostensibly reading English literature and Italian, and he even went to lectures "with all those pustular, sweaty, hockey-playing, earnest, big-breasted girls"; but he found his real interest in the Oxford University Dramatic Society. Nevill Coghill—don, critic, and man of the theatre—was directing *Measure for Measure*. When Burton asked for a part, Coghill said he was sorry but the play was all cast. Burton's native aggressiveness flashed to the surface. "Let me understudy the leading man," he said wickedly. "Undermine" would have been a better word. When *Measure for Measure* opened—with people like John Gielgud and Terence Rattigan in the audience, for the O.U.D.S. was as important then as now—guess who was striding the boards as Angelo?

Well, heaven forgive him! and forgive us all!
Some rise by sin, and some by virtue fall.

WHEN JENNY LIND entered New York Harbor on a paddle-wheel steamer in 1850, P. T. Barnum went out in a rowboat to greet her, carrying a spray of red roses in his arms. She was a plain young woman of twenty-nine, hair parted in the middle. Her nose was a Nordic spud. She had a wide mouth, and she wore no cosmetics. She was the most celebrated operatic soprano in the world.

Barnum was tone-deaf. But he had brought Jenny Lind to America because he hoped to change his image. When people thought of Barnum, they thought of sheer bazazz, while he wanted them to think of fine arts. This cost him a down payment of a hundred and eighty-seven thousand five hundred dollars before the Swedish singer would set foot on board ship. His investment paid off in cash if not in dignity, as Jenny Lind made a twelve-thousand-mile, hundred-and-sixty-five-concert sellout tour during which a single seat went for six hundred and fifty-three dollars. Another time, a thousand standing-room tickets were sold in fifteen minutes. The press went insane. Every other line might have been written by Barnum. *Holden's Dollar Magazine* said, "Sell your old clothes, dispose of your antiquated boots, distribute your hats, hypothecate your jewelry, come on the canal, work your passage, walk, take up a collection to pay expenses, raise money on a mortgage, sell 'Tom' into perpetual slavery, dispose of 'Mose' to the highest bidder, stop smoking for a year, give up tea, coffee and sugar, dispense

with bread, meat, garden sass and such like luxuries—and then come hear Jenny Lind."

She sang Mozart, Weber, and Meyerbeer, offset by such additional items as "Comin' Thro' the Rye" and "The Last Rose of Summer." Presenting a little-known song from an opera called *Clari*, she immortalized "Home, Sweet Home." Her voice spanned nearly three octaves, topping out at G above high C. Her high F sharp was pure, and she had an incredible ability to sing very softly at that altitude. No one could match her messa di voce—the technique of holding a single note while increasing and diminishing its volume. She did it as if she were twirling a knob. It is possible that some of this was wasted on numbers like "Old Black Joe," but she always sang parts from the operas in which she had won her fame, from *Norma* to *Lucia di Lammermoor*.

Washington Irving went down the Hudson to hear her, and was vastly impressed. So, in Boston, was Henry Wadsworth Longfellow, who declared, "She sings like the morning star." Even Niagara Falls fell at her feet as she stood on a projecting boulder and sang an aria to the plunging cataract. Stephen Foster, of Pittsburgh, a young Northerner in love with the South, was forever grateful to her because she added his songs to her repertory, including the one she called "Mein Old Kentucky Home." Nathaniel Hawthorne thought she was dull.

When Jenny Lind arrived in Washington, President and Mrs. Millard Fillmore hiked through the woods between the White House and the Willard Hotel to leave their calling card. She began her first Washington concert before an audience that included the Fillmores, Senator Thomas Hart Benton of Missouri, Henry Clay of Kentucky, and fourteen empty seats in the

front row, reserved for the seven members of Fillmore's Cabinet and their wives, who were at the Russian ministry soaking up vodka. Jenny Lind was singing "Hail, Columbia" when they swayed down the aisle and took their seats. Daniel Webster of Massachusetts, Secretary of State, stood up potted and sang along with her, while his wife tugged furiously at his long black tails.

When Jenny stayed with friends in Denmark, Hans Christian Andersen would come around to tell stories to the children of the house, a pretext for seeing her. He fell in love with her. He wrote "The Nightingale" for her. When she was cold toward him, he wrote "The Snow Queen." When he begged her to marry him, she silently handed him a mirror. That night, he wrote "The Ugly Duckling." Gladys Denny Shultz, the author of *Jenny Lind: The Swedish Nightingale*, offers a modified version of this famous anecdote. She claims that Lind really meant to impugn her own appearance, arguing that it is beyond belief that Lind could be that cruel.

Jenny Lind's circle included Berlioz, Meyerbeer, Schumann, and Brahms. Her great friend Felix Mendelssohn loved to sit at his piano and explore her upper register. Frédéric Chopin referred to her affectionately as "this Swede." She often rode along the trails of Wimbledon with the seventy-eight-year-old Duke of Wellington, who decorated his dotage with bright young ladies of the stage. Crowned potentates of the Continent, from Prince Metternich of Austria to King Frederick William of Prussia, competed for her friendship. She was a favorite of Queen Victoria. After Jenny Lind died, in 1887, at the age of sixty-seven, a memorial was inscribed to her in the Poets' Corner at Westminster Abbey—the first time in the Abbey's history that a woman had been so honored.

The Athapaskans are not much impressed that a young Princeton graduate on a prospecting adventure in the Susitna Valley in 1896 happened to learn, on his way out of the wilderness, that William McKinley had become the Republican nominee for President of the United States.

This sentence and several that followed it in *Coming into the Country* unexpectedly provoked an angry and bitter letter from a woman in Oregon. The passage in the book continued:

In this haphazard way, the mountain got the name it would carry for at least the better part of a century, notwithstanding that it already had a name, for uncounted centuries had had a name, which in translation has been written, variously, as The Great One, The Mighty One, The High One. The Indians in their reverence had called it Denali. Toponymically, that is the mountain's proper name.

The reader in Oregon railed vitriol at me and called me by names other than my own. She expressed thorough contempt toward anyone coarse enough even to hint at the thought of calling the mountain by a name other than McKinley. The mountain, she said, had been named by her late father.

What was I going to say to that?

I wrote to her on the stationery of the Council of the Humanities, Princeton University, and thanked her, and warmly congratulated her, and told her that I am the father of four daughters and it would be my fondest hope that someday, in some situation, after I am gone, one of them might rise up as nobly in defense of me.

(But I still think the mountain should be called Denali.)

BRIGHT AND NERVOUS, frenetic, full of quick smiles and dark moods, shouting "Onward, onward" between laughs, performing in a cashmere sweater, always tieless, Mort Sahl manages to suggest barbecue pits on the brink of doom. Holding a rolled newspaper in his right hand, with flashing blue eyes and a wolfish grin, he states his theme and takes off like a jazz musician on a flight of improvisation—or seeming improvisation. He does not tell jokes one by one, but carefully builds deceptively miscellaneous structures of jokes that are like verbal mobiles. He begins with the spine of a subject, then hooks thought onto thought, joke onto dangling joke, many of them totally unrelated to the main theme, until the whole structure is spinning but is nonetheless in balance. All the time he is building toward a final statement, which is too much a part of the whole to be called a punch line, but puts that particular theme away.

When Little Rock Central High School entered the news, Sahl approached the subject from various byways, one of which was his fondness for sniping at President Eisenhower. A critic had said that if the President were really a man he would take a

little colored girl by the hand and lead her through that line of bigots into the high school. "That's easy to say if you are not involved," Sahl said. "But if you are in the Administration, you have a lot of problems of policy, like whether or not to use an overlapping grip." Wild laughter always greeted that one, but— with a nod and a nervous chuckle and a characteristic "It's true, it's true"—he would slide off into a skein of digressions, usually with an aside for interested conservatives, telling them that they could get the *Chicago Tribune* anywhere in the United States "flown in packed in ice." Then, circling back toward Arkansas, he would press on to the famous line that put Little Rock into absolute focus. "I like Governor Faubus," he admitted. "But I wouldn't want him to marry my sister."

While politics is always the trunk line, his humor ranges everywhere. Crazes craze him. His piece on the hi-fi ends with a family living in their garage and using the house as a speaker. Psychoanalytic clichés are seldom spared. Once, he says, a bank robber slipped a teller a note saying "Give me your money and act normal." The teller replied, "First, you must define your terms. After all, what is normal?" Some of Sahl's jokes are even more rarefied. Once, he began talking about a student in a statistical-analysis course who would never use sigma but preferred his own initials instead. When someone laughed, Sahl looked up in surprise, and said, "If you understand that joke, you don't belong here. You had better call the government at once; you are desperately needed."

Mort Sahl was born on May 11, 1927, in Montreal, where his father kept a tobacco shop. Although that might suggest a solid burgher background, Canadian citizenship, and perhaps a fall on the ice, Mort had none of these. His father had come out

of an immigrant family on New York City's Lower East Side with a strong will to be a playwright. Broadway and Hollywood gave him just enough encouragement to make him sure that he had the art, but his failure to make a living in his field turned him into a dark cynic, whose philosophy functioned in the tight spectrum between "It's all fixed" and "They don't want anything good." Mort's mother, on the other hand, was an intractable optimist. On this trampoline Mort was raised, an only child, soaking up skepticism and idealism, respect for creativity and contempt for show business. The family moved to Los Angeles, where Mort's father found a job as a clerk for the F.B.I. From the age of two and a half, little Mort liked to stand behind the radio and shout through it his own version of the news. At eight, he hung around radio stations, picked up discarded scripts from the floor or out of garbage cans, and read them into a dummy microphone he had made for himself at home.

Living in Berkeley, unemployed, he became the academic equivalent of a ski bum. Auditing classes off and on, he drank a ton of coffee a month in all-night campus snack bars, argued art, social science, and politics into the abstract hours. He slept mainly in the back seat of his moldering Chevy, and ate cold hamburgers provided by a Nietzsche-soaked friend who worked in a short-order restaurant. From the wooden microphone of his childhood to the hamburgers with Nietzsche relish, he accumulated experience, intelligence, and enmity, until just one more shattering blow was needed to complete his training. He got it after a pain developed in his lower right side and a doctor at a Berkeley hospital referred him elsewhere because he lacked the four hundred and fifty dollars

for an emergency operation. The doctor ran after him demanding ten dollars as an examination fee. Sahl's appendix ruptured. He recovered in a veterans' hospital, and the American Medical Association joined his repertory. His mildest joke about the medical world suggests that "the A.M.A. opposes chiropractors and witch doctors and any other cure that is quick."

Late that fall (1953) he arranged an audition before a live audience in San Francisco, at the lower-case, lower-depths hungry i (for intellectual). On stage, Sahl began talking about the McCarthy jacket, explained that it was like the Eisenhower jacket except that it had "an extra flap to go over the mouth," and added that "Senator McCarthy does not question what you say so much as he questions your right to say it." No one even smiled. Then up from the bar came a muscular laugh—from Enrico Banducci, the proprietor of the hungry i—and Mort was in, at seventy-five dollars a week.

He built his original audience of students who came in from the University of California and other regional campuses. Soon his following increased to multitudes with no such common denominator. He calls his followers "my people." Many have peach fuzz on their cheeks, and many have it on top of their heads. What they share is a fondness for articulate irony and a sense of being "in." Now and again, someone gets up and walks out muttering "Communist." Others think him too brash and offensive, a nihilist, a hater of everything. His people see him as the black knight of the implied positive— an idealist whose darkly critical moods really imply a yearning for perfection. They will all understand the words of a college freshman who says, "He has a cool way of digging deep."

FOR THE GENERAL ELECTRIC PAVILION, architects turned a huge dome inside out, revealing a supporting lining of inter-sticed steel, so that the building's over-all look suggested tripes à la mode de G.E. In the tops of metal trees, I.B.M. set what appeared to be a fifty-ton egg in a nest of plastic. Johnson Wax suspended a huge gold clam over a blue pool inside six slender white pylons that rose high and flared in unearthly petals. The General Motors Futurama was built around the idea that the human population—two-thirds of the way through the twenti-eth century—had ample room in which to explode, and proved the thesis with models of future machines and future cities, to be built in trackless wastelands. A G.M. machine a couple of hundred yards long would soon subdue the rain forest. Out in front of it, smaller machines would run around felling trees with laser beams. Blink, blink. The red beams sliced the trees and they toppled. The great mother machine now took over, moving forward to eat the trees and all the understory, mean-while extruding four-lane highways from its distant rear. Cities sprang up in the bush to either side.

HE ONCE DESCRIBED HIS LIFE as "a succession of fortunate circumstances." He was in his twenties then. More than half of his life was behind him. His memory of his mother was con-fined to a single image: in a blue corduroy bathrobe she stood in

a doorway looking out on the courts and playing fields surrounding their house, which stood in the center of a Richmond playground. Weak with heart disease, she was taken to a hospital that day, and died at the age of twenty-seven. He was six.

It was to be his tragedy, as the world knows, that he would leave his own child when she was six, that his life would be trapped in a medical irony, as a result of early heart disease, similar to his mother's.

His mother was tall, with long soft hair and a face that was gentle and thin. She read a lot. She read a lot to him. His father said of her, "She was just like Arthur Junior. She never argued. She was quiet, easygoing, kindhearted."

If her son, by legacy, never argued, he also was schooled, instructed, coached not to argue, and as he moved alone into alien country, he fashioned not-arguing into an enigma and turned the enigma into a weapon. When things got tough, he had control. Even in very tight moments, other players thought he was toying with them. They rarely knew what he was thinking. They could not tell if he was angry. It was maddening, sometimes, to play against him. Never less than candid, he said that what he liked best about himself on a tennis court was his demeanor: "What it is is controlled cool, in a way. Always have the situation under control, even if losing. Never betray an inward sense of defeat."

And of course he never did—not in the height of his athletic power, not in the statesmanship of the years that followed, and not in the endgame of his existence. If you wished to choose a single image, you would see him standing there in his twenties, his lithe body a braid of cables, his energy without apparent limit, in a court situation indescribably bad, and all he does is put his index finger on the bridge of his glasses and push them

back up to the bridge of his nose. In the shadow of disaster, he hits out. Faced with a choice between a conservative, percentage return or a one-in-ten flat-out blast, he chooses the blast. In a signature manner, he extends his left arm to point upward at lobs as they fall toward him. His overheads, in firebursts, put them away. His backhand is, if anything, stronger than his forehand and his shots from either side for the most part are explosions. In motions graceful and decisive, though, with reactions as fast as the imagination, he is a master of drop shots, of cat-and-mouse, of miscellaneous dinks and chips and (riskiest of all) the crosscourt half volley. Other tennis players might be wondering who in his right mind would attempt something like that, but that is how Ashe plays the game—at the tensest moment, he goes for the all but impossible. He is predictably unpredictable. He is unreadable. His ballistic serves move in odd patterns and come off the court in unexpected ways. Behind his impassive face—behind the enigmatic glasses, the lifted chin, the first-mate-on-the-bridge look—there seems to be a smile.

THE PUN ALSO RISES, even while maligned as the lowest form of humor. In good hands, words can be made to jump, molt, wiggle, shrink, flash, collide, fight, strut, and turn themselves inside out or upside down. Like many writers of light verse, Felicia Lamport is fond of creating new words by lopping off prefixes, but she does it better than most:

Many a new little life is begot
By the hibited man with the promptu plot.

Images glisten under her rhymes.

And what could be moister
Than tears from an oyster

Mocking the Age of Publicity in an essay which notes that where writers write has become almost as important as what they write (Thomas Wolfe scratched out his manuscripts on refrigerator tops; Jean Kerr worked in the front seat of her Chevrolet), Lamport tops them all with Elihu Linot, who always wrote on the backs of women, starting at the neck and working down. His editor eloped with a manuscript. There was no carbon.

NORTH AMERICAN MENSA, a club for people of superior intelligence, held its Annual Gathering the other weekend at the Biltmore. To join Mensa, candidates must prove, through tests, that they have higher I.Q.s than at least ninety-eight per cent of the rest of humanity. Mensa was founded in Britain in 1946. North American Mensa was not established until 1960, but it has become the largest subdivision of the organization, with more than ten thousand members in the United States and Canada. Mensa cannot be called leftist, rightist, uppist, downist, in, or out, for its constitution forbids any declaration of opinion on a Mensa-wide scale. Mensa's aim is simply to bring together the brightest people in the world, so that their brains may interact to the benefit of themselves and humanity gener-

ally, and so that they may feel less lonely as they follow their otherwise separate paths.

Naturally, I felt complimented when I was invited to lunch with the Ms and FeMs at the Mensa A.G. Mensa people speak in a marvellously unbent, unfolded, unmutilated syntax that draws heavily on initials. An M is a Mensa member who is male. A FeM is a Mensa member who is female. There is a young-adult Mensa group called YaM. The A.G. is the Annual Gathering. And a sign at the entryway to the Palm Court of the Biltmore, under the clock, said, "This way if you have P.A.I.D." I arrived at eleven-thirty, to find that a morning business meeting—closed to the press—was still in session in the Madison Room, next to the Palm Court. Explosive shouts were coming from inside. I learned later that S.I.G.R.I.M.—a Seriously Interested Group for Reform in Mensa—was in there hacking away at the parliamentary defenses of the Establishment. One of S.I.G.R.I.M.'s several grievances was that the leadership had denied S.I.G.R.I.M. the right to call itself a Special Interest Group, so S.I.G.R.I.M. had been forced to settle for Seriously Interested Group instead. I could not see into the room, but I heard one man bellow "Point of order!" five or six times and another propose a new faction, to be called S.I.E.G. H.E.I.L. A large man came out of the room looking exasperated and said, "Every nut in New York is in there. They voted on a resolution, and forty per cent of them don't know what they voted for."

Pretending not to notice, I began to look through a variety of Mensa publications that were set out on tables in the Palm Court. One fact sheet noted that there were ten thousand two hundred members, "of whom seven thousand five hundred and eight are male; two thousand six hundred and eighty-nine are

female; and there is no information on the remaining three Ms."
In *Charisma: The New York Mensa Literary Review*, I read a
poem called "Icelandia," beginning "Iceland is a nice land to live
in," and a poem called "Interrupted Cliché," which is here given
in its entirety: "Of all the sorry works of men, the sadist." A geographical breakdown of the Mensa membership listed Maine,
Vermont, New Hampshire, Massachusetts, and Rhode Island as
the states of New England. Connecticut and northern Virginia
were included in the Middle Atlantic category. ("Our statistical
system is new," an M later explained. "There are still a few bugs in
it.") I learned that fifty per cent of the Mensa members are college
graduates. In the "Personals" column of the June, 1966, *Mensa
Bulletin*, I read, "Avid Ray Walston fan seeks M support in all-
out effort to save 'My Favorite Martian,'" and an ad that said,
"M—28, tall, lean, and considered handsome. Spent last few
years travelling the world and I'm tired. College grad, athlete,
loves all the beautiful things in life and is an incurable romantic.
Is there a FeM somewhere in the vicinity who is good-looking,
honestly sincere, and fed up with the average man?"

I wondered what was going to come out through that door
when the business session ended and the group moved to the
lunch, in another room. My first guess—angry, bearded, fistic
geniuses—had given way to a vision of bleached poets. Then,
suddenly, they came—something over two hundred and fifty Ms
and FeMs, the assembled members of North American Mensa.
There were men in cord jackets, women in pastel summer suits,
pretty young girls with long, silky hair, people who looked to
me like salesmen, engineers, students, housewives, schoolteach-
ers. Unless one happened to know the truth, one would never
have suspected that extraordinary reservoirs of intelligence un-
derlay their familiar and reassuring appearance.

The lunch was served at large round tables—appropriately, for the name "Mensa" is meant to suggest that the group is a round-table society of equals. They came not only from New York but also from California, Wyoming, Virginia, Massachusetts, New Mexico. There was a carpet salesman from Louisiana, with his wife, and a woman who teaches English at Seton Hall University; an installer of computers; several computer programmers; two Canadian college students; several high-school students; an electrical engineer. On my left was a man who is the chief engineer of a rubber company in New Jersey; he is an M.I.T. graduate and recently moved east from Akron. On my right was a Yale sophomore, and next to him was a management consultant. The Yale student told me that there are Mensa activities going on in New York City almost every day— hikes around Manhattan, study groups in Esperanto and Chinese, a Mensa lunch in a different restaurant each day of the working week. On Thursdays, the restaurant is the Playboy Club. The consultant, who wore black-rimmed glasses and had a fine-line mustache, sensed the presence of a non-M. He turned to me and said, "Are you here in a reportorial capacity?"

"Yes," I said, feeling my status plunge and go on plunging until it bottomed out at the twentieth percentile.

"This is a really heterogeneous group," the consultant said. "The only thing we have in common is our intelligence level. You don't meet anyone who's weird. You don't meet anyone who's crazy. We are a giant conversational community. We talk about any idea, on any subject. We're vociferous not only about internal Mensa problems but also about philosophy, mathematics, education, art, psychology, history, and religion. If you're intelligent, your interests are not limited to one field. Mensa is the only organization that selects its members by a scientific process, but you wouldn't know a Mensa member if you passed him on the street. We are like everyone else. Intelligence doesn't show in the face or the personality. I saw a man this morning in Grand Central who looked lost and dishevelled, and I said to myself, 'There's a real idiot.' I saw him an hour later here at the Mensa meeting. He's an M."

I asked the consultant what had attracted him to Mensa.

"I saw an ad in a newspaper," he said. "I have always had an aversion to joining organizations, because it is possible to get into one and six months later find it migrating to Moscow. But, constitutionally, that can't happen in Mensa. Curiosity brings most people into Mensa. They wonder what it would feel like to go into a room full of intelligent people and hear them talk. Mensa people are very discreet about their I.Q.s. They never compare them. I feel that I myself would have done better if there had not been mosquitoes in the room when I took the test. The intellectual doesn't have a place in society. He's homeless. He's rootless. Mensa is about the only home base for intellectuals, excluding the university environment. Some people use universities for the same purpose, or professional colleagues, but these sources are very limited."

The keynote speaker of the day was Isaac Asimov, the Boston University biochemistry professor who writes science-fiction novels, and he proved on this occasion to be a first-rate stand-up comedian. The keynote was a series of jokes, some of which he told twice. He said he imagined that all the people in the room—put together—were brighter than he was. He explained evolution to them in fresh terms; it was really survival of the weakest, for the fish left the ocean not because they were ambitious but because they were crowded out.

More speakers and much discussion followed, through the

afternoon. "It's a pleasure to talk to a group that is representative of the I.Q. elite," one speaker said. "The structure of society discriminates against people of extraordinary intelligence. Society expects intelligent people to be strange, then creates the circumstances that guarantee this will be true." There was some laughter, a bit of applause.

An M spoke up sharply from the floor. "Are you suggesting that we hide our light under a blanket?" he asked.

CLICK. THE NINE BALL plops into the side pocket, the cue ball hits one cushion and stops near the center spot. Big as a water tower but light on his feet, with a diamond ring on a pudgy finger, the fat man moves around the table. For thirty-one consecutive hours, with an almost incredible repertory of massé shots, bank shots, gather shots, and combinations, with just enough English and the right amount of draw, he has been defending his reputation as the best there is. He chalks up and shoots again. Click. The fifteen ball slams into the corner and disappears. Minnesota Fats is still the greatest pool shark in the world.

Jackie Gleason does his new job with remarkable ease. He memorizes at first sight. While Method actors search their souls and "live" their roles, Gleason riffles through a script and is ready to go. His fellow performers both amuse and irritate him with their warm-up exercises. While shooting *The Hustler*, Paul Newman was forever shaking his wrists like a swimmer before a race. Now, on the set of *Requiem for a Heavyweight*, Anthony Quinn shadowboxes and dances up and down—

"marinating," as Gleason puts it—for half an hour before a take. Gleason stands around cracking jokes and shouting, "Let's go! Let's go!" But his directors uniformly report that when they call for action, Gleason snaps instantly into the character he is playing.

HER VOICE WAS CLEAR, vibrant, strong, untrained. She wore no makeup, and her long black hair hung like drapery, parting around her long almond face. In performance, she came on, walked straight to the microphone, and began to sing. No patter. No remarks. She usually wore a sweater and skirt, or a simple dress. Occasionally, she affected something semi-Oriental that seemed to have been hand-sewn out of burlap. The purity of her voice suggested purity of approach. She was only twenty-one and palpably nubile, but there was little sex in that clear flow of sound. It was haunted and plaintive, a mother's voice, and it had in it distant reminders of madrigal singers performing at court, and of saddened Gypsies trying to charm death into leaving their caves. "Barbara Allen" was one of the set pieces of folk singing, and no one sang it as achingly as she did. From "Lonesome Road" to "All My Trials," her most typical selections were so mournful and quietly desperate that her early recordings would not have been out of place had they been played at a funeral. She added some lighter material to create a semblance of variety, but the force of sadness in her personality remained compelling.

Her mother was English-Scottish, her father was born in Mexico. His academic track as a physicist took him to Los

Angeles, Buffalo, Baghdad, Boston, and Paris. Along the way, their three daughters learned some memorable lessons in bigotry. When Dr. Baez was doing military research in Buffalo, for example, the family thought it would be a pleasant experience to settle in a small and typical American town. They chose Clarence Center, New York, population nine hundred. Their next-door neighbor was a senile old man who scowled at Joan's dark skin and said, "Niggers." The Baezes called the neighbor Old Bogey. To keep Old Bogey confused, they sank a plug spout into a telephone pole outside the house and hung a bucket on it. Dr. Baez picks up the narrative. "We knew that he would be full of contempt for our supposed ignorance of maple tapping, but we knew that he could not resist peeping into the bucket. We were in stitches of laughter, peeping from our window when he would come by, look around furtively, and peek into the bucket. Then we began to put things in the bucket—water and so on. He was astonished. Poor Old Bogey."

In Redlands, California, Joan found a situation that cut deeper than one old crank. The Hispanic schoolchildren there played in separate groups from the "whites." Observably, the dominant tone of her personality changed from ebullience to melancholy. Her thirteenth birthday came, and she said something she would repeat often: "Mummy, I don't want to grow up."

She spent a month or so at Boston University studying theatre—the beginning and end of college for her—and she met several semipro folk singers who taught her songs and guitar techniques. She never studied voice or music, or even took the trouble to study folklore and pick up songs by herself. She just soaked them up from those around her. She sang in coffee-houses in and around Harvard Square that were populated by the Harvard underworld—drifters with Penguin Classics protruding from their blue jeans, and no official standing at Harvard or anywhere else. They pretended they were Harvard students, ate in the university dining halls, and sat in on some classes. Joan Baez—who would long be thought of as a sort of ethereal beatnik because of her remote manner, long hair, bare feet, and burlap wardrobe—actually felt distaste for these academic bums from the start. She said, "They just lie in their beds, smoke pot, and do stupid things." They were her first audiences, with real Harvard students and general citizens, who grew in numbers until the bums were choked out. She was often rough on them all. When one patron lisped a request to her, she lisped in reply. When another singer turned sour in performance, Baez suddenly stood up in the back of the room and began to sing, vocally stabbing the hapless singer on the stage into silence. In the summer of 1959, another singer invited her to the first Newport Folk Festival. Her clear-lighted voice poured over the thirteen thousand people there and chilled them with surprise. Recording companies closed in. A representative of Columbia Records—dropping the magical name of Mitch Miller, the star-making artists-and-repertoire man—said to her, "Would you like to meet Mitch, baby?"

She said, "Who's Mitch?"

THOMAS WOLFE WAS an undisciplined, ungovernable American Conrad whose sea was the land of his birth. His words, seeking "to find language again in its primitive sinews," rioted onto paper in millions, growing out of him, over him, and sometimes beyond him. In the West a few years before he died,

Wolfe saw a sequoia for the first time. He stared upward for a moment in unbelieving silence, then ran to the big tree, his long arms stretched wide. It was a boyish gesture, but this man of thirty-five still believed that he might draw into his embrace the biggest thing that lived.

He strode along in his size-thirteen shoes, embarrassed by his six-foot-six-inch, two-hundred-and-forty-pound frame, carrying his eccentricities with him until fame had transformed them into folklore. He seldom washed, changed his shirt, or had a haircut; he could live for hours, even days, on cigarettes and coal-black coffee, then swallow twelve eggs, two quarts of milk, and an entire loaf of bread in one breakfast. Wild-eyed and forever talking with all the intensity of his written prose, he sprayed everyone in range with reservoirs of spittle from the corners of his mouth. Some thought him ludicrous, but thousands worshipped the ground his feet never quite touched. Sooner or later he accused all his friends of tormenting him, but he needed them badly, and once, at a party in his new Manhattan apartment, he reached to the ceiling with a black crayon and wrote, "Merry Christmas to all my friends and love from Tom."

GOVERNMENTS OF THE WORLD have long found it convenient to bury their gold in Manhattan. The site is five thousand three hundred and twenty paces due south of the Public Library, then two thousand two hundred and eighty paces due west, and it is betokened by the topographical configuration of an old and now obscured streambed in Maiden Lane, whence the route proceeds straight down into the earth until, fifty-five feet below sea level, one enters a grotto jackhammered out of solid metamorphic rock and there finds the gold. The hoard has become, as far as is known, the largest quantity of gold that has been accumulated in one place ever. It is a sixth of all the gold that has been mined during the history of the world. The limestone palazzo overhead is the Federal Reserve Bank, which serves as the custodian of the gold, although the United States' share of the total is under a hundred million dollars' worth—around half of one per cent. Just knowing all that gold is there produces a sensuous need to be in its presence, a certain stir in the lower coin.

The Fed resembles a men's club with unusually high dues. Wood fires burn discreetly. Art from the Metropolitan Museum is hung in the galleried corridors. Washrooms are full of combs, brushes, clothes brushes, dental towels, doctor scales. One instinctively spruces up before being ushered into the presence of the gold. I stopped first in an upstairs office to see Thomas O. Waage, a senior vice-president, whose Cash Custody Department has physical responsibility for money of all kinds within the building, including bullion. He said that things would be very quiet down at bedrock, because gold was not, except in a more or less religious sense, backing anybody's currency anymore. There might be more gold than ever down there, but it was doing less. As a base of currency, it no longer had any practical meaning. In the old days, when gold was gold, the gold deep under the Fed was literally moved about in support of the currencies of nations. Suppose Denmark owed a large sum of money to France. A coded cable would arrive from Copenhagen and another from Paris, with matching instructions from each country. Then, down in the gold bins, professional stackers—men with forefingers the size of bananas from the handling of bars of gold—would go into Denmark's compartment and take out what was owed to France. They would wheel it to the French compartment and stack it inside. That sort of thing went on all the time. If, say, Argentina paid a debt to Britain, or Indonesia paid one to Kuwait, gold was lugged from one stack to another deep under Manhattan, which is why so many nations—about sixty in all—wanted to keep gold in one place. The work was so exhausting that the stackers functioned in units, like lacrosse midfielders or hockey lines, going in and out of action every few minutes. They wore magnesium covers over their shoes. A bar of gold was only seven inches long, but it weighed four hundred troy ounces.

The price of gold traded on the free market had long since come unstuck from the official price agreed upon in international monetary circles, and between the two prices a gap had grown that had widened beyond the point of absurdity. The official price now, the "official" value of gold as the underpinning of currencies, was forty-two dollars and twenty-two cents an ounce. The price of gold on the free market—jewelry gold, industrial gold, gold of private hoarders—was approaching two hundred dollars an ounce. This difference had paralyzed the great treasures below us. At the official price, no one, obviously, was going to use gold to pay a debt, nor were many nations psychologically prepared to fling their gold into the free market, receiving paper, even huge amounts of paper, in return. Forces of atavism, mysticism, primitivism still apparently combined in the human soul to give spiritual status to this metal. So now it sat in limbo—fourteen thousand tons of it, anyway—deep in a man-made cave.

The mouth of the cave, its only entrance, is plugged with a

steel cylinder that weighs ninety tons. When the cylinder is turned, it presents an opening large enough to walk through. A whole team must go in if anyone goes at all. I, for example, after I left Mr. Waage, was taken down to the bedrock level by Richard Hoenig, an assistant vice-president of the bank, and we were met at the steel cylinder by Edward Hood, of Cash Custody; by Albert Nyland, of the Vault Division; and by Sam Ludman, an auditor. No one ever goes into the presence of the gold unaccompanied by a trio from the Auditing, Vault, and Cash Custody divisions, who, among other things, supervise the gold stackers. On any number of doors, including the hundred and twenty-two doors of the gold-storage compartments, there are three locks, the keys or combinations of which are separately held in the pockets or memories of people from the three divisions. To avoid collusion, assignments are rotated, so that no threesome works consistently together. "It's my gold," Hood said, by way of explanation. "I keep it in Al's house, and Sam handles it." Among them, these three had worked in the bank ninety-four years. "You eventually come down to this job," said Sam.

"We go down the ladder instead of up," said Al.

"The next step is to be buried," said Ed.

We stepped through the steel and into the cavern. The predominant color in there was dull yellow. The architectural ambience was early cellblock. The place might have been a county jail. Visible through the steel mesh and the steel dowels in the doors of the cells were stacks and stacks of sullen, imprisoned gold. A thousand bars or so were lying around on pallets outside the cells, evidence that all activity had not stopped. Switzerland, for example, has a law that a certain ratio must be kept constant between amounts of paper money and amounts of gold on hand in Switzerland, so the Swiss occasionally call for gold from their bin in New York. I reached for a bar of gold and picked it up. It was a bit smaller than an ordinary construction brick. It weighed twenty-eight pounds. It lacked lustre—in fact, it appeared to be a lead brick borrowed from a radiation lab and painted with gold dope. Its markings indicated that it was 99.94 per cent pure. It was worth, officially, about seventeen thousand dollars and could bring perhaps seventy-five thousand in the free market. I felt a tendon preparing to snap in my shoulder, and I put the gold down.

"Be sure to call it a bar, not a brick," Mr. Hoenig said. "Everyone who works down here is sensitive and touchy about having them called bricks."

National identities were secret. I peered into various numbered cells, wondering whose gold was sulking there. I saw a bar that was marked with a hammer and sickle, but that could have been anyone's by now; it had been cast in the Soviet Union in 1937. The value of the contents of each compartment was written on a tag on the door. No. 3, for example, contained fourteen thousand five hundred and sixty-eight bars, worth, officially, about two hundred and fifty million dollars—the hoard of a modest client. Accounts might range from under a hundred thousand dollars to five or six billion dollars, Hoenig said. Each compartment represented all or part of an individual account, for the gold of different customers was never commingled.

The stacks had been put together with both the care and the pattern that masons would employ in the making of a dry wall—level courses, shimmed (with wood), interlocking. In one large compartment was well over half as much gold as there is in Fort

Knox. It was in three separate stacks. Two were about fifteen feet high and included a hundred thousand bars apiece, while the third had been built with fifty thousand bars. Stackers—sweating, working like the slaves of pharaohs—could handle a maximum of twelve hundred bars a day, so the construction of these three stacks alone had taken nearly a working year.

Suddenly, the composite foolishness of all this shivered through history and fell on me like a ton of gold. I thanked everybody and split for sunlight. Suffering from acute duodenal aurophobia, I staggered into the street.

THERE IS A CONVENTION in musical theatre called the Girl's First Song—that first number in which the heroine states who she is, what she wants, and hints at the perils that might befall her, such as "A Cockeyed Optimist" from *South Pacific* and "Wouldn't It Be Loverly" from *My Fair Lady*. In *Funny Girl*, Barbra Streisand stands under the marquee of a theatre and declares in her first song:

> *I'm the greatest star,*
> *I am by far,*
> *But no one knows it.*

From that moment, no one has a chance not to know it. "I'm a great big clump of talent," she sings with conviction. "I've got thirty-six expressions—sweet as pie to tough as leather—and that's six expressions more than all the Barrymores put together. I'm the greatest star—an American Beauty rose, with an American beauty nose."

This nose is a shrine. It starts at the summit of her hive-piled hair and ends where a trombone reaches pedal B flat. The face it divides is long and sad, and the look in repose is the essence of hound. But as she sings number after number and grows in the mind, she touches the heart with her awkwardness, her lunging humor, and a bravery that is all the more winning because she seems so vulnerable.

When the lights go up for intermission, people dive into the *Playbill* to find out about Barbra Streisand. They don't learn much. In the biographical notes, Barbra remains onstage. She wrote them herself. Her young life's work has been to elevate and sculpt her own archetypical personality, and no string of drab printed facts is going to get in her way. She reveals that she is an accomplished bead stringer and a collector of old shoes, born in Madagascar and reared in Rangoon. Her pharaonic profile and scarab eyes more nearly suggest Aswan. In truth, she was born and raised in Brooklyn, between Newtown Creek and the Gowanus Canal.

More than willing to forsake her anonymity, she nonetheless feels the pain of its loss. People who recognize her in the street and ask her for autographs make her uncomfortable. Some of these people wear their hair in the lofted way that she does, and attempt to replicate her glassy, communicant look, for she is a godhead of their private reveries. Others who stop her are just impious strangers. Seeing her tasseled yellow blouse showing through under a South American skunk coat, her white wool slacks and dirty sneakers, they will say, "Hey, you look like Barbra Streisand!"

THE AGE OF OARED SHIPS lasted three thousand years, and the largest of them were built closer to the beginning than to the end of that span of time. Ships with single banks of oars took the Greeks to Troy. Biremes transported the Phoenicians. Eventually, toward the end of the sixth century B.C., triremes developed. A hundred and twenty feet long and with a twenty-foot beam and three coordinated banks of oars, the trireme was the most sensible expression that this form of naval architecture would ever be given. With the Battle of Salamis, the brief, extraordinary era of the super-galleys began: quadriremes, quinqueremes, decaremes, dodecaremes—even tredecaremes, with eighteen hundred men at the oars. Huge, high-sided, millipede ships, they rammed one another out of existence. The largest oared ships in history were two trigintaremes, constructed in the third century B.C. by King Ptolemy II of Egypt. Soon after that, according to the historian Callixenos, Ptolemy IV built a quadragintareme, but scholars consider Callixenos untrustworthy and doubt whether such a ship ever existed. The trigintaremes were awkward enough. With thirty banks of oars sticking into the water like roots into the earth, they had the over-all mobility of banyan trees. The trend reversed. Before long, most Mediterranean navies were back at least to quinqueremes. The Romans, for the most part, used biremes and triremes, and one of Mark Antony's many troubles at Actium may have been that he had with him a fleet of outmoded decaremes. A millennium passed. The nautical merchants of Venice were still using three-bank ships in the thirteenth century, and the Venetian vessels had almost exactly the same dimensions as the early Greek triremes.

Secretary of Defense Robert McNamara has announced that the Lockheed Aircraft Corporation is going to build by far the biggest airplane ever designed. The C-5A, as it is called, weighs three hundred and fifty tons. In 1948, when the B-36 was introduced, newspapers printed scale drawings that showed Orville Wright's plane taking off from one wing of the B-36 and landing on the other, a hundred and twenty feet away—a hundred and twenty feet being the distance of the first controlled flight. A flight the length of Orville Wright's could occur inside the C-5A. The great nose of the plane swings up and open, on hinges, like the visor of a knight's helmet. It allows more cargo room within the fuselage, which is two hundred and thirty-six feet long, and the plane can be taxied with its visor open. Large buses could drive into the plane two at a time. Six of them could fit inside with space to spare. Its engines are so big that one of the pods they fit into could easily be converted into a cottage. The plane itself is so big that when the pilot pulls on the control stick, there will be no immediate perceptible response. Many seconds later, the nose will start to rise.

THREE HUNDRED YEARS AGO, a notion was a thought. This meaning endures, but now the word also signifies all the miscellaneous objects on department-store notions counters. It is uncertain how this small fork in a minor etymological stream came to exist, but it is possible that John Locke created it all by himself when he wrote, in 1690, "Essences of the Species of mix'd

Modes are by a more particular Name call'd Notions." Locke was thus not only a father of modern democratic government but also a father of modern retailing, for Notions Departments are what make department stores go. The theory is that customers drawn in by the essences of the species of mixed modes on the main floor will proceed to higher floors and more ambitious purchases.

Notions, in the world of American retailing, were once pins, needles, ribbons, buttons, bows, and related products. Pins, in the United States, were first made in Rhode Island, and out from there went Yankee peddlers, who became known as notions peddlers, and who sold needles, pots, pins, and pans in villages across New England and, eventually, on the frontier. A standard opening used by a peddler was "Can I suit ye today, ma'am? I've all sorts of notions." After 1849, "notions vessels"— bazaars afloat—began appearing in San Francisco and elsewhere on the California coast. In the nineteenth century, the notion to end all notions was the bustle. An 1888 issue of *Fabrics, Fancy Goods and Notions* described one bustle as being made of muslin-covered wires that "cross each other to form an excellent spring, allowing the bustle to close easily as the wearer is seated, and promptly resuming its shape upon arising." By the eighteen-nineties, notions counters had become standard features of stores everywhere in the country. Some pins and needles can still be found on notions counters, but notions today are anything at all that will sell—preferably items with some sort of real or pretended novelty. Notions buyers have become the biggest barracudas in the department-store world. When something really good comes along in, say, Housewares, a Housewares buyer who tries to get near it will probably be chewed up by the superfish from Notions.

I **WENT DOWN** to Washington to observe the ritual distribution of fifty thousand dollars to six civil servants—tax-free, and with scarcely a string attached. The money was venerable, as money goes, not the sort that is tossed around in packets. It had once belonged to John D. Rockefeller III and had been further aged on the books of Princeton University. Rockefeller and Princeton have been doing this for twenty years. Rockefeller felt so sorry for civil servants during the era of the witch hunts that he sought a way to stimulate their morale, and since not even John D. Rockefeller can just hand cash to a public servant without setting off a sprinkler system somewhere, he gave Princeton stewardship of the money and asked the university to set up a program to select recipients. Virtually unknown outside the government, the awards carry more prestige (and far more money) than any other award given to members of the Civil Service. Departments nag for them, compete like football teams. Defense will call up Princeton, flash a little first-strike capability, and ask after the chances of this or that Defenseman. Commerce buzzes analogously. State skips diplomacy. Meanwhile, hundreds of letters have gone out from the university to people in and around the government, asking for detailed nominations. Anyone at all can write a nominating letter without being asked. The result is a list of about a hundred and twenty-five nominees a year—the best among the people Franklin Roosevelt described as having "a passion for anonymity."

Luna Leopold, as a recipient, seems particularly to epitomize what the Rockefeller awards are about: the singling out of a government worker of no nonsense and stunning competence, the strong suggestion that he is not unique but one of a kind, the concomitant revelation that someone is noticing, even cheering, what he is doing. Leopold, of the United States Geological Survey, is a hydrologist, a world authority on river mechanics—a name from an inner page of a newspaper, if ever there at all. With a single report, though, he may have saved the Everglades. Dark, tall, a falcon, he appears to have been stolen from a wall in the Prado. He knew just why he was being honored. "It is a good thing Rockefeller is doing," he said, over drinks. "No one in the middle echelon actually thinks that he himself will get the award, but the fact that someone gets it makes everyone feel his job is more important. The public has lost confidence in government and in people who work for the government. Rockefeller is saying that somebody thinks federal service is a good thing. There's a hell of a lot of good work done in the government."

A winner once went straight to the nearest dealer and bought a Cadillac. Rockefeller could not care less what happens to the money, as long as the winners keep working for the government. Before being confirmed by Princeton's trustees, they are asked to declare that they have no immediate plans to retire. That is the one string attached.

I GUARDED HIM once in a while in the noon basketball game in Dillon Gym. He didn't go to his left, and he didn't go to his right, but he easily managed to get off shots. The cigar may have helped him, the blown smoke. The cigar crazed me on the tennis court as well. We played regularly through the summers, and he was better than I was eight times out of ten. As I struggled against him and went down to defeat, in the middle of his face there was always that stump—contemptuous, glowing. If the cigar disappeared, I felt a shiver in the bones, knowing I was playing over my head.

One very hot summer evening, near dusk, while Jadwin Gymnasium was under construction, I called his house, and asked for him, and his wife said, "He isn't here. He's down at the new gym." The new gym was a large hole in the ground, girders rising. "The what?" I said. And she said, "The new gym. He goes there every night. He communes with the new gym. If he has to be away from town, he sends one of us."

I dropped whatever I'd been doing, bought two sixteen-ounce cans, drove to what is now the Jadwin parking lot, and walked in the half-light toward the skeleton of steel. He was sitting on the retaining wall between Caldwell Field House and the construction site. As I approached him and sat down beside him, he neither looked at me nor said a word. I handed him a can and he opened it. He continued to say nothing. He just gazed into the interior of the future gym. I was not about to speak, I can tell you. If anybody broke his silence, he was going to do it, not me. For a very long time, he said nothing and he never glanced my way. It could have been half an hour. The sky was all but dark. Finally, without turning his head, he said, "Can you imagine putting a bad basketball team in there?"

I told that story to Dan White, who used it as the opening anecdote in his 1978 book, *Play to Win: A Profile of Princeton Basketball Coach Pete Carril.*

One year, a basketball player submitted an adroitly written and charming essay in application for my spring-semester writing course, which would begin on February 1st. I picked up the telephone and called Pete.

"One of your basketball players has applied to my course and I'd like to take him but it's an all-afternoon seminar and I'm not going to take him if he has to get up and leave and go to the gym."

In Pete's only tone of voice—his gust-driven toad baritone—he broke in and said, "What's his name? What's his name?"

"Matthew Henshon."

"He can do it. He can do it. What time does your class end?"

"Four-twenty."

"He can do it. What's more—let me tell you—if that fucking kid ever walks out early, if he ever misses so much as one minute of your class, he will never play another minute of basketball for Princeton."

Henshon was a starter on a championship team.

Now that I no longer play tennis, I see Pete much less often, and therefore look forward all the more to talking with him and catching up with him on the long fast walks we sometimes do together from Jadwin. Evidently, he looks forward to these occasions, too. As we go down the towpath, he has earphones on his head and listens to bullfight music.

My editor Bob Bingham called me at home and said that a friend of his at Vogue *had asked him to see if I would write a very short piece on birds for a very long sum of money. I said I knew nothing at all about birds, they had the wrong man. Bingham said, "We*

mustn't let the money out of the family." I reemphasized my lack of qualifications. Bingham said, "Just interview me." I said, "O.K.," and added, graspingly, "if you'll accept half." We talked for a time and I recorded what he said. I figured if I was going to take half the money, I had to contribute something, however briefly. Plumbing my memory for a personal lead, I began, as follows, to write.

SITTING IN A CANOE on a small, wild lake in the northern-most part of New Hampshire, I saw a bird leave the shore. I could not tell what it was, but from a distance it seemed to have the configuration of a gull. It was flying low over the water, and directly toward me, like a Grumman Avenger making a run. It had no more than two feet of altitude. Without swerving, it came steadily on, with an obvious sense of target. The distance closed to a hundred yards. Fifty. Twenty-five. God knows what the creature thought the boat was, or what I was, but a collision was now imminent, and I raised my arms in self-defense. Sud-denly the bird lifted its head, spread its wings, and, with its body straight up, stopped dead in the air. A huge pair of eyes. In them, a look of miscalculation. An owl. We stared at each other, faces a foot apart. With a whip of wings, it was overhead and gone.

As soon as I could, I got to a telephone and called my bird-watcher. He said it was too bad that the owl had chosen some-one who might not sufficiently appreciate the encounter. That was true enough, for I suffer from a kind of congenital opacity to birds. My wife knows and loves birds. I have many friends who know birds. I have long felt somewhat guilty that I lack not only knowledge but also understanding of birds, and of what draws people to them. My bird-watcher is a business associate of mine whose name is Robert Bingham. I have never understood him, either. I began, some time ago, to try to draw out of him the essence of what makes him watch.

Mr. Bingham is a tall, rufous man with unsuspicious eyes. He has the ample sort of mustache that all creation, even a bird, would trust; and he has thought deeply on the pleasures and advantages of bird-watching. "One might as well be blunt about it and concede that the entire enterprise is redolent of sexuality," he said. "The voyeurism is embarrassingly obvious. I mean your stealth, your luck, and a couple of ground lenses can bring you into a secret intimacy with some of the most beautiful, graceful, and sensual beings in nature. The perspective is unreal—it's as if you were up there on a branch among the leaves with them, and you cease to be your earthbound self entirely for a bright, timeless flight as you strain to catch one more glimpse of the golden-crowned kinglet darting through the conifers. Did I really see that crimson streak running through the yellow cap, or did I imagine it? The excitement can be compared only to that I experienced as a fourteen-year-old gulping my way through *Lady Chatterley's Lover*, looking for the dirty parts. And yet the fantasy is of an exquisitely purer intensity—the eroticism of angels, not of thrashing animals on the ground. If I were to become a bird in some reincarnation, I would choose to be a cardinal. The cardinal is a rather common fellow, actually—a run-of-the-mill suburban-commuter type, despite the bright red suit. But have you ever looked closely at his wife? Damnably attractive, to my way of thinking. Just my type. A simple but superbly tailored dress in a kind of bronze color with a warmth that grows on you the more you look at it. A stylish long tail, with which she lets you know that, while she comes from an old family and went to the best schools, there's plenty of spirit to her. And those lips! A luscious orange you can scarcely believe is natural. They have a nice pouting fullness to them, without the exaggerated clownishness of her cousins the grosbeaks. Cardinals are very uxorious, you know. Stay together all winter, not just in the breeding season. I can see why. A few weeks ago, I saw a couple giving each other pumpkin seeds at one of my feeders. Sexiest performance I've ever seen."

Mr. Bingham insists that he is "a more or less average bird-watcher" and that a review of his motivations might go far toward explaining what makes people in general stand around in the woods with field glasses, trying to add to their life lists. There are more than six hundred bird species known on the North American continent. With "accidentals" and subspecies, seven hundred and two are listed in Roger Tory Peterson's *A Field Guide to the Birds*—a standard text that, for many, has been supplanted by the Golden Press's *Birds of North America*. Fanatics, the sort who go out at the height of the migration to do a "century run" (one hundred birds in a day), have been able to do six hundred or more in one year.

I once asked Mr. Bingham how long his life list was.

He said, "I will not say. I deplore competitiveness."

"In what sense, then, are you an average bird-watcher?"

"Well, for example, with a field guide in hand, I can probably differentiate half a dozen of the warblers when they are in full breeding plumage in the spring. To me, they are the most glorious objects of the hunt. The black-and-white has a natty salt-and-pepper topcoat, for instance; the magnolia has black spots down a splendid yellow vest. But I am completely lost among what even the guidebooks call 'confusing fall warblers,' who have suited up and shed their mating plumage and look all alike."

"How long have you been birding, Mr. Bingham?"

"I find the word 'birding' affected. It is used by new-style ecologically minded counterculture participants who, being ashamed of the prissiness of all the little old ladies in tennis shoes who preceded them, feel they have to talk tough about what they are doing. They make me uncomfortable. I'm as determined as the next nature lover that our rivers shall be pure, our air uncontaminated, and our primeval forests preserved from brutish developers. But, somehow, the romantic escapism of bird-watching has been driven out by all the new ecological zeal. The last time I went on a bird walk, it was led by a perfectly wonderful young man who spent most of his time talking about solid-waste disposal."

"How long have you been bird-watching, Mr. Bingham?"

"I came to it fairly late—that is, in my thirties—after a lifetime of ridiculing bird-watchers. It was during a vacation on Martha's Vineyard, where the Chilmark Community Center sponsored bird walks every Monday morning. I had heard that the leader of the walks, Edward Chalif, could lead his groups past no-trespassing signs to parts of the island a casual visitor would never see. That first Monday morning I was completely entranced. I mean, it was as if I had discovered that a whole other world—of beautiful, sentient beings—was superimposed on the familiar world I had been living in for thirty-some years. I could suddenly see it, almost get into it—into another dimension of experience that I might otherwise have missed entirely. I was shown three warblers that I hadn't known existed. Chalif taught me the devices by which I attract birds to come to me, instead of footing it aimlessly through the woods after them. What I do is first make a noise like a hunting screech owl, then make a noise like a hurt baby robin. If done well and in a promising neighborhood, the act brings them flocking in by the dozens to find out what the hell is going on. The owl noise is made by getting a fair amount of spit collected in the mouth on top of the tongue, tilting the head back, and whistling low several times. The hurt-baby-robin noise is made by kissing the back of your own hand vigorously."

"Have there been triumphs in your bird-watching career?"

"There is a large tree outside my kitchen windows in Dobbs Ferry. Into the bark, I press suet and other meat fat during the winter. One morning, as I walked into the kitchen to put the kettle on for coffee, an immense woodpecker—unmistakably the pileated—flapped its way across the yard and landed on the tree for breakfast. I did not dare cry out the news to my family for fear of scaring the bird away; but when I had quietly summoned my wife, three children, and a Newfoundland dog, the pileated woodpecker was still there. I once positively identified a razor-billed auk sporting in the waves off the inlet to Lake Tashmoo on Martha's Vineyard, the day before I was to leave the island. I called Eddie Chalif to tell him about it. A year later, I heard Chalif tell a group that he had once been able to take thirty people to see a razor-billed auk off Lake Tashmoo—on the basis of a tip he had received the summer before from a man whose name he couldn't remember."

"What—if any—are your main handicaps as a bird-watcher, Mr. Bingham?"

"I can't remember the names or the salient characteristics of the birds. I once had the difference between the least sandpiper and the semipalmated sandpiper down pat. The last least

I saw I called a sanderling. The titmouse, which crawls downward on my tree eating suet, is a bird whose name I can never remember. 'What's the name of that upside-down bird?' I will ask my wife, who is not a bird-watcher. 'Nuthatch, dummy,' is her reply."

ALONG THE WAY we stopped at Geysir, where a great hole in the ground is the world's eponymous geyser. The old geyser is no longer forthcoming. It is full of water but not of action. It had literally been roped off. Close at hand was a young geyser. At five- to seven-minute intervals—no more than that—it swelled tumescently, let forth a series of heavy grunts, and into the sky shot a plume of flying steam. Meanwhile, the old geyser just sat there, boiling. We learned how—on special occasions—Icelanders make the old geyser do its thing. They throw soap into it, and it erupts.

Moving on, we passed a waterfall of the size of the American Niagara, and then we drove for an hour or two on the gravels of an outwash plain that was covered with rounded boulders and no vegetation, not so much as a clump of grass. Eventually, the car could go no farther, so we left it behind and proceeded north on foot. There was a stream to ford. Laura had running shoes and I had boots. She got onto my back and I carried her across. We then walked a couple of miles, also on rounded rocks, and up onto a high moraine, where, coming over the crest, we looked down into a lake backdropped by cliffs of blue ice. This was the edge not of a valley glacier but of an ice cap covering nearly five hundred square miles. Above the lake, the ice wall rose about a hundred and fifty feet, and was sheer. There came sounds like high-powered-rifle shots, as huge bergs calved away from the ice cap and plunged into the water. There was no going farther. On the way down the moraine and back toward the river ford, I attempted to increase my credit line by mentioning that glacial rivers grow in the afternoon with the day's melt from the sun, and this time we could expect a larger river when I carried her across it. But this time she was having none of me. Apparently, she had forded her last river on her father's back. She took off her shoes and negotiated the stream.

THE LIBERTY SCIENCE CENTER'S declared purpose is to combat what it sees as a general scientific illiteracy, to strike a spark in children in obvious and subtle ways, and then to draw them back and keep the spark aglow—ultimately, to educate many and, with luck, to inspire a few. And how does a museum do that? In the words of the management: "First, don't scare them off."

Up a ramp I go, fearless, and into the four-level atrium, my youth camouflaged by a gray beard. The escalators have glass sides and visible working parts. They carry you up to the Insect Zoo—to colonial displays of carpenter ants, Kenyan millipedes, pink-toed tarantulas, and emperor scorpions. Close by, second graders are digging in a mound of dirt in search of weevils, pill bugs, springtails, scorpion-fly pupae, centipedes, and small local millipedes. Don't scare them off.

The African millipedes are longer than hot dogs and call to

mind segments of BX cable. Would I like to handle one? In this company, what choice do I have? Nina Zitani, of the museum staff, lays a Kenyan millipede on my open palm. Curled like an ammonite, it covers the palm. "In a minute," says Nina, "she'll begin to move."

She begins to move. She uncurls, stretches from my wrist to beyond my fingertips—her touch as tentative as an art restorer's brush. She seems self-conscious. Understandably. People say she is a millipede, but she has only two hundred and fifty legs. Leaving my hand, she crawls onto Nina's.

Would I like to hold a Madagascar hissing cockroach?

My nod is meant to suggest that this has been a lifelong ambition.

Madagascar hissing cockroaches, with their inquisitive and wormlike antennae, are flat and hard and about three inches long. They hiss because they think you are going to eat them. As I fondle one's chitin, the roach responds with the sound of a printer printing. The roach is covered with crawling mites. What the egret is to the Texas longhorn, the mite is to the Madagascar roach.

Central American cave cockroaches thrive behind glass on a walnut limb. The adults are three to four inches long. Their pronouncedly segmented babies are scattered about them like horseshoe crabs. Not by accident are cockroaches, in such taxonomic variety, the star attractions here. This is Greater New York—roach utopia.

Stand in front of the thermographic sensing camera. Your mottled image appears on a screen in colors relating to the surface temperatures of your body. That's me! A perfect likeness: green beard, yellow mouth, pink nose, red head. The body's surface-temperature range can vary through thirty degrees. As I stick out my tongue, it licks like a white-orange flame.

At the Bernoulli Bench, you can pick up an air hose, blow it over the top of a ball in a cylindrical cage, and make the ball rise. You toss Ping-Pong balls and they stick like burrs to the sides of air jets you cannot see. You blow a jet between two bowling balls. Instead of scattering, they slam together. Bernoulli's principle shapes the airfoil and lies behind the breaking baseball. Daniel Bernoulli was the Swiss mathematician who discovered, in the eighteenth century, that pressure is inversely related to the speed of moving air. Since air pressure acts from all directions, air flowing rapidly across the top of an object will make the pressure there lower than the pressure that is acting on the bottom and the sides. Enjoy your flight.

At the Stream Table, across the way, water flowing over crushed walnut shells forms oxbow bends and braided rivers, making point bars and cut banks while you watch. The staffer at the spigots is not the Carl Sagan of the earth sciences. He says he has been given to understand that the subject he is presenting is known as geomorphology and mentions offhandedly that he is a member of the California bar. His knowledge of limnology is about what you would learn in a torts course.

In an aquarium of streaming water, you try to control various objects through the glass with magnets—page 1, line 1, fluid dynamics.

The idea behind the museum's various discovery rooms is that if something especially arrests your interest, you can take it further. There are twenty-five staff members on each floor, ready to help you assemble bones, deconstruct a wasps' nest, or work on a CPR doll. Equipment is here (the scanning electron microscope) that is not in most schools. In the discovery rooms, whether children are digging for weevils or disassembling computers, they are, in effect, making their own exhibits. They bring their toys or machines from home to the basement Swap Shop—things for taking apart. They bring their dichroic reflectors, their capacitors and reed relays, their pop pumps and solenoids, and exchange them for hard-drive air filters, pancake motors, electromechanical scissors, and portable throwing stars.

As for me—the over-all effect on me—if I were ten years old, not even the feathery caress of a six-inch Kenyan millipede could coax forth a scientist from within; it would, on the other hand, tickle the hell out of the writer there.

A PERSON WHO SPECIALIZES in handheld altimeters will always know how high he is but may have difficulty keeping his bearings. This I learned in Fort Tryon Park, near the north end of Manhattan Island, from William Peet, of Allenhurst, New Jersey, an engineer trained at M.I.T., who has pretty much cornered the American market in high-precision pocket machines that disclose one's altitude with respect to sea level. If Peet has a mission, manifestly it is not to replace the magnetic compass but to offer a supplement—an additional bit of gear with a utility of its own—for those who walk in wild terrain.

Fort Tryon Park essentially consists of two conical hills, which range in elevation from about thirty feet to two hundred and fifty. They are steep and, in places, sheer. On one summit is the Cloisters, medieval outpost of the Metropolitan

Museum, surrounded by descending woods. Peet dropped from sight there, among the trees. When he came back half an hour later, he handed me a topographic map that he had marked with an X. He said he had hidden a miniature Statue of Liberty at the X, and challenged me to find it. I had a compass, and spurned, for the moment, supplemental instruments of any kind. With map in hand, I departed.

From the northeastern corner of the Cloisters, Peet's X was on a bearing of 44 true. Nothing to it, I thought. Just follow that bearing and look for the statuette. I followed the bearing and looked over an abyss. Large outcrops of Manhattan schist buttress the hill. Forty-four true involved suicide, and I wasn't prepared to make a commitment. Deciding instead to approach the incline from below, I went down a circuitous path to the bottom of the park, where I emerged from the natural woods and entered a grove of plane trees protruding from the asphalt of a playground, where children were sliding and swinging and climbing on jungle gyms under small steepled roofs. The playground was in the acute angle formed by Riverside Drive and Broadway over the Dyckman Street Station of the A train. This intersection serves the Thirty-fourth Precinct as Times Square serves the Fourteenth. Inwood Liquors. The Cloisters Café. A McDonald's with a large American flag reefed a few turns around a horizontal pole.

McDonald's proved to be the best base point for a shot through the playground and back into the woods. Peet's X was now on a heading of 272—close to due west of the Chicken McNuggets. Compass in hand, I followed the bearing back across Broadway, back across the playground from tree to target tree, then into the rising forest. There was much understory—bushes, thick vines—to break through. I broke into leafy, cavern-like spaces full of Smirnoff bottles of pint size, beer cans in brown bags, some coconut husks, and condoms. There were enough foam cups to suggest a football crowd. There were a couple of pillows almost as large as mattresses and in remarkably good condition. I found a doorless fireproof safe, so heavy I could not budge it. I found the door, forty feet away, uniformly dimpled in shapes of crowbar. When I came to a twelve-foot stone retaining wall, I left a Tropicana carton at the foot of the wall, went around the obstacle, returned on the uphill side, and followed the bearing to a height that made no sense. I found no statuette. I returned to the streets to choose another vector.

I walked down Payson toward Dyckman and turned around. On the topographic map, Payson happened to be lined up like an arrow pointing at Bill Peet's X. I took the bearing—222—and retraced my steps. I climbed a five-foot wall and kept going, rising through the trees until I reached the crosshairs of the X. I leaned down to pick up the treasure, but none was there.

I bushwhacked to the summit, where an infinite number of Japanese men came out of a stretch limo and filed into the Cloisters. Sagging to a bench, I admitted frustration. Peet looked patient and pleased. Peet is a tall, quiet man who wears studious glasses. He was also wearing a short-sleeved print shirt. The print was a large-scale map of a small part of Maine. Spreading before me an array of altimeters, he said, "Try these."

I chose one for each hand. I chose a Model 88, good to eighteen thousand feet, temperature compensated, with a sixteen-jewel shock-resistant movement, its face scarcely two inches in diameter but designed and calibrated to present with clarity any of nine hundred twenty-foot increments, at each of which it is accurate. I also chose an electronic altimeter, known in steep places as the Ultimeter, whose digital display, in a case 2.7 inches square, presents its elevation in ten-foot jumps.

Peet told me to go down the path until I was between sixty and fifty feet above sea level, then leave the path and go off to the right on a contour through the woods. Before long, I would come to a fallen tree, and then ...

"To the right?" I asked.

"Yes," said Peet.

With respect to the path, I had just spent an hour looking to the left, where the legs of his X crossed.

As if they were votive offerings, I bore the altimeters in upturned palms while making the descent. Steadily, the 88's needle moved. Nervously, the Ultimeter jumped back and forth from level to level but generally took the plunge. This was not an airplane descending through five thousand feet on its final approach to Newark. This was cutting it fine. These altimeters were positioning a human being in distances not much greater than from a ceiling to a floor. A hundred and forty. A hundred and twenty. A hundred feet. I almost stumbled, tumbled down the hill. My eyes wouldn't leave the machines.

Just below sixty, where the needle of the Model 88 rested confidently while the numbers in the Ultimeter kept jumping from fifty to sixty to seventy and back, I made my move. I left the path and headed off to the right through the steep woods, keeping the numbers steady, hewing to the contour. I came upon the fallen tree. I stayed on the contour and found the statuette.

"With an altimeter, each contour line is a position line,"

Peet remarked after I staggered up the hill for the last time. "It is an extra dimension in land navigation."

A person could go around, say, a ravine and reach a destination while walking on a level. To walk on a level requires a tenth as much energy and time as descending or ascending steep grades, Peet said. When you're on a mapped trail somewhere, an altimeter will tell you what contour you're on, and therefore where you are and how far you have to go. In steep country, dense foliage, fog, darkness, blinding snow, you do not need to see landmarks—as you do with a compass—to find your way. Traversing a mountainside, you follow a contour and avoid lateral drift, which can throw you off-line as you sight with a compass from tree to tree to boulder. You can use an altimeter to retrieve game. If you shoot a leopard, you can note its elevation, and go back and seek it at that altitude. Birders in Hawaii have found elusive species by learning the altitudes where they nest. Geologists looking for gold in Idaho last summer acknowledged that their altimeters were the most precious instruments they carried, and were indispensable in heavy timber. The exploration companies insisted that every rock sample be marked with an elevation. If a rock tested positive, they would need to return to the source. For want of an altimeter, they might repeat the legend of Lost Dutchman's Mine.

My mind developed lateral drift. I saw myself using altimeters for purposes of which Peet may not have dreamed. What is the altitude of John McGillicuddy, the C.E.O. of Manufacturers Hanover Trust, at his desk at Forty-eighth and Park? (One hundred and thirty-five feet.) What is the altitude of John Reed, the chairman of Citicorp, Fifty-fourth and Park? (Seventy-five feet.) Where is the highest lawyer in New York?

(Arnold Schickler, World Trade Center, twelve hundred and seventy feet.) Where is the lowest lawyer in New York? (In every precinct.) What is the altitude of Kathleen Battle, Sixty-fourth and Broadway? (A hundred feet and rising.) What is the altitude of Leona Helmsley, Federal Courthouse, Foley Square? (Fifty feet and falling.) How many buildings rise above the two-hundred-and-fifty-foot line? Two hundred and fifty feet—a calculated, data-based guess—is where the ocean will top out when the ice of Antarctica and Greenland melts. In the history of the earth, only three times has ice appeared in great sheets over the land: in a relatively brief episode six hundred million years ago, in another brief episode three hundred million years ago, and in the ice of the Pleistocene now. These anomalies aside, through forty-six hundred million years nearly all the water on the earth, which is a fixed amount, has been liquid. With an altimeter, we could go around and see who's going to make it when things return to normal. At two hundred and fifty feet above the present sea are the nineteenth floor of the Empire State Building, the twenty-first floor of the Chrysler Building (which stands in a hollow), the nineteenth floor of 30 Rockefeller Plaza. The Metropolitan Museum will not make it, the Metropolitan Opera will not make it, the Cloisters will not make it. The south hill in Fort Tryon Park will rise above the water as a tiny island three feet high.

Fort Tryon Park. "You were saying?" I said to Peet.

Peet was apologizing about his misplaced X. He had been so confident of his map reading in that small area that he took no bearings when he made the X.

It was a benign mistake, for in so doing he was able not only to demonstrate the utility of his small machines but to make another point, too: Never go into the trackless woods unless you have a compass.

. . .

[A 2018 amplification: For field geologists recording the elevations of outcrops, altimeters are superior to GPS if they are calibrated and the barometric pressure is not changing.]

AN UNKNOWN MOVIE ACTOR checked into an English hospital and took a couple of dozen scripts to bed with him. He is unknown because he has so far appeared in only three minor pictures. He had the scripts with him because producers all over the world are nonetheless begging him to work for them. He needed hospitalization because he is physically shot. During the past twenty months, he has suffered sand burns on his feet, sprained both ankles, cracked an anklebone, torn ligaments in his thigh and hip, dislocated his spine, broken his thumb, partially lost the use of two fingers, sprained his neck, and suffered two concussions. The survivor's name is Peter O'Toole, and he is Sam Spiegel's Lawrence of Arabia.

TO BECOME INTERNATIONAL FILM STARS, Europeans once had to learn English, and all the Marlene Dietrichs, Paul Munis, Charles Boyers, Ingrid Bergmans, Peter Lorres, and Maurice Chevaliers did so. But now it is different. As ruins go,

Hollywood is smoking more and enjoying it less, while the most renowned motion pictures of the present are being made by Europeans and Asians. Hence there is a new phenomenon—the movie idol who is adored throughout the United States in much the same way that Clark Gable was once admired from Saipan to Tangier. The greatest of these is Marcello Mastroianni.

His handsome face, young in its outlines but creased with premature wrinkles, has a frightened look, as of a mantis who has lost faith in the efficacy of prayer. He suggests the antithesis of Renaissance man—painfully aware of nearly everything, truly able at nothing. His spine seems to be a stack of plastic napkin rings. But he has no false bravado, and he is relentlessly attractive. In nearly every woman there stirs the same silent response: "Marcello obviously needs professional help, but first he needs me."

Marcello has so often been cast as himself—he was actually called Marcello in Federico Fellini's *La Dolce Vita*—that he went eagerly for his role as a Sicilian nobleman in *Divorce Italian Style*, which gave him a chance to grease down his hair, grow a mustache, and decay even more.

THE PHONE RINGS. The man who answers is lower middle-aged with a lower middle paunch. He looks something like a nearsighted kipper.

"Ell-ow," he says in pure cockney.

"Is Peter Sellers there?"

"'E aynt eer. Ooze callin?"

Peter Sellers is there, of course, at his flat in London, and he is on the line. Contentedly, he clicks down the phone. Shy men like Sellers hate to talk to friends, let alone strangers. Sellers is the world's best mimic, equipped with an enormous range of accents, inflections, and dialects—including five kinds of cockney, Mayfair pukka, stiff-upper BBC, Oxford, Cambridge, Yorkshire, Lancashire, West Country, Highland Scots, Edinburgh Scots, Glaswegian Scots, Tyneside Geordie, Northern Ireland, Southern Ireland, French, Mitteleuropa, American twang, American drawl, American snob, Canadian, Australian, and three kinds of Indian. He fools everybody. Everybody but his friends. They are wise to him. When they call him up and a sweet old German nanny answers, they say, "Come off it, you old bastard." The trouble is that there really is a sweet old German nanny at Sellers's place, and she often gets an earful when she answers, "Voss diss?"

Sellers is the son of vaudeville troupers. He has been a performer since the age of two, and he spent his youth acquiring every sort of face but one of his own. He became a brilliant actor by painful necessity, since he is by nature diffident, introspective, and not particularly articulate unless he is pretending to be someone else. He once said, "I've got so many inhibitions that I sometimes wonder if I exist at all. I have no desire to play Peter Sellers. I don't know who Peter Sellers is, except that he's the one who gets paid. Cary Grant is Cary Grant—that's his stock-in-trade. If I tried to sell myself as Peter Sellers, I'd be penniless. Write any character you have in mind and I'll shape myself to what you have written. But don't write a part for me."

Sellers builds characters out of people he knows or seeks

out, getting ready for new roles by fastening himself to the real article—union leaders, neurotic Americans, old generals—and absorbing their personalities down to the last tic. The result is always funny, sometimes merciless. But when he reads a new script, Sellers usually panics. "Better ring up and say I can't do it," he tells his wife. He paces frantically for hours. "Then," she says, "Peter buys a new car and he's all right." In the past fourteen years, he has owned sixty-two automobiles. One was a Rolls-Royce Silver Cloud, but it made him uncomfortable. He put a classified ad in *The Sunday Times*: "Titled motor car wishes to dispose of owner."

JOSEPH MARTIN, computer methodologist at *The New York Times*, has been pursuing for some years what he describes as "the ideal philosophy of creating a newspaper." According to the ideal philosophy, you start by "capturing the keystroke at the origin." Keystroke? The reporter, at the typewriter, hits the original keystrokes of a story. Martin aims to absorb them electronically, retain them in a computer, and eliminate all the laborious and manifold retypings that now occur as a piece of writing makes its way, typically, from reporters through bureaus to the home office to the desks of editors and eventually to linotype machines. The ideal philosophy also calls for the elimination of the typing paper that writers write on, which is regarded as an unnecessary and archaic encumbrance. Following suggestions of reporters and editors, and with the help of an electronics firm in Westchester, Martin has coaxed into being a device that can actually do all this.

The *Times* is just up Forty-third Street from *The New Yorker*. When I arrived to have a look at Martin's device, the third-floor newsroom was in a state of routine cacophony: a large open space as aswarm with bodies as the floor of a stock exchange, copy paper in motion everywhere, copy editors looking like physicists with crooked cigarettes and feral eyes, reporters hugging telephones or already down in the trenches—sporadic bursts of typing. The machine that was going to tranquillize this scene was locked away in a quiet cubicle. I was led to it by Joe Martin, a slim and somewhat solemn man with a graying crew cut, and by Socrates Butsikares, an editor with decades of experience on various news and feature desks, who now coordinates editorial-staff interests with those of the rest of the company and is thus deeply involved in the electronic innovation. A big man, Butsikares wore a bright yellow shirt, and there were lemons on his tie. We were joined as well by Israel Shenker, who is an old friend of mine and is one of the *Times*'s bright-star reporters and most skillful writers. Shenker had not previously seen the machine that was designed to change his world.

At thirty-two pounds, it rested heavily on a table. Resembling a small blue suitcase, it was eighteen inches by thirteen by seven. It would fit under an airline seat. Its name was Teleram P-1800 Portable Terminal. Butsikares unpacked it. Its principal components were a TV-like cathode-ray tube and a freestanding keyboard that had the conventional "qwertyuiop" arrangement of a typewriter keyboard plus flanking sets of keys that had designations such as SCRL, HOME, DEL WORD, DEL CHAR, CLOSE, OPEN, and INSRT.

Butsikares plugged the keyboard unit into the TV-screen

unit, sat down, and began to write. As his fingers fluttered, words instantly surfaced on the screen, up to forty-four characters per line:

> Washington, D.C.—President Ford said today
> that he would no longer ask the Congress to
> soak the poor while his fat-cat rich friends
> take away the wealth of the Republic.

"Now, suppose you want to get a little color into this," Butsikares said, and he began tapping keys—marked with arrows pointing up, pointing down, pointing sideways—around the HOME key. A tiny square of light, known as the "cursor," began to move up the face of the tube. It was something like the bouncing ball that used to hop from word to word in song lyrics on movie screens. It climbed to the first line, then moved left until Butsikares stopped it in the space between "Ford" and "said." He tapped the INSRT key. He then wrote:

> who was wearing his faborite blue suit and his soup-
> stained blue tie,

The new words came into the space after "Ford," and to accommodate them the cursor kept shoving to the right all the other words in the sentence. They went around corners and down the screen. Butsikares moved the cursor until it rested upon and illuminated the "b" in "faborite." He pressed the DEL CHAR (delete character) button, and the "b" vanished. He replaced it with a "v." "Now, suppose you want to take a word out," he said, and moved the cursor to the word "away."

"All the cursor has to do is touch any part of the word," he went on. "Then you hit the DEL WORD key, and it's gone." Away went "away," and the words to either side moved to within a space of each other. Similarly, the cursor could—if directed to—eat whole lines, whole paragraphs. "What you have written is not set in cement," Butsikares said. "You can change anything easily. If I had my druthers, I'd rather write on this thing than on any typewriter I've ever seen."

When the screen fills (it holds about a hundred and twenty-five words), the writer just keeps going. For every new line that comes on at the bottom, a line disappears at the top. To go back and look things over, just hit the SCRL key. The whole composition will roll backward or forward like a scroll. In blocks of some three hundred and thirty words (a little less than half a *Times* column), the developing story is transmogrified into sound frequencies and drawn off into a cassette. If the writer needs to see what is in the cassette, that, too, can be brought back to the screen. At the end, after the cursor has made its final tour through the text to help polish up the prose, the reporter goes to the nearest telephone. The P-1800 contains couplings that will fit over the telephone's earpiece and speaker, and the reporter straps these into place, then dials 212-556-1330, the computer's number. At three hundred words per minute, the P-1800 sends words as bleeps to Forty-third Street. If the story is, say, seven hundred and fifty words long, the computer has it all in a little over two minutes. An editor, sitting at an "editing terminal," can then call for the story and see it instantly. The editor's machine is much like the reporter's—a rolling scroll, a dancing cursor. The editor can perform extensive changes, condensations, paragraph-shufflings, and meddle muddles, but the editor *can never destroy one word of the writer's copy*, because deep in its tissues—Butsikares is now assuring Shenker—the computer will preserve the original version "until Hell freezes over." While the temperature is dropping, though, the editor's version goes into the newspaper, because the computer stores both, and it is the editor, in the course of things, who ultimately presses the button that causes the computer to set the type that readers will read. The story—written by a reporter and then fed through wires, transistors, and brains—has been fussed with along the way but never recopied.

"Try it, Shenk," Martin said.

"It's a new world, Shenk," Butsikares said.

Shenker, wearing a dark, neatly tailored pinstriped suit, looked less like a reporter than like a banker being approached for a loan. He sat down, shot his cuffs, and addressed his fingers to the P-1800. Butsikares and Martin watched expectantly. Shenker wrote smoothly, swiftly, and without hesitation, his words lighting up on the screen. He wrote:

Israel Shenker doesn't think that this is
the answer to gunpowder.

"It is easier to work with than paper," Butsikares said. Shenker kept going, words leaping to the screen:

It may replace the electric train as a gift
to youngsters at Christmas.

"The machine saves half an hour on deadline," Butsikares told him. Reporters would no longer have to call in stories and dictate them to tape recorders, as many do now, trusting transcribers to retype them correctly on paper.

Shenker went on writing:

The machine could be useful if it allows one
to sleep later or get to the office late.
But my considered judgment is that if we got
up a half hour earlier or worked a little
harder we wouldn't have to strain our
muscles carrying around a large machine and
searching for a harder way to do a story.

"This is only a test model. They cost five thousand dollars apiece, and we are not placing our full order until the weight is down to around twenty-three pounds."

Then again, this is an ideal machine for
editors. It will prolong their joy at the
spectacle of reporters struggling with
something that they don't understand.

Squat and bull-shouldered, Butsikares had the appearance of a lineman some years retired from a defensive platoon. "If you take a device like this out with you and you find you don't like it, Shenk, don't use it," he said. "You have to ask yourself, 'What am I trying to do? What am I covering? Is time of the essence? Will the machine help?' It is perfect for wars, riots, golf matches, conventions. Gordon White has already used it to cover three football games, including the Cotton Bowl, and he would have missed deadlines if he hadn't had it."

Shenker went on typing:

> I suppose the only thing this machine won't
> do is eliminate editors. Let us have a
> machine that gives the reporter his due.

Shenker at last sat back. "Have you tested this for radiation?" he said.

"Yes," said Butsikares. "You can be a father."

"You can write on it, but you can't think on it," Shenker commented. "It would be great for Mozart, who used to compose in his head and then write what he saw there, but not for me." Struck with an afterthought, he went back to the keyboard:

> Do not wire until you see the flights of
> their whys.
> Do not sire until you flee the plights of
> their lies.

"Shenk, if someone had come to you once saying, 'Listen, kid, I've got a great machine—it will do away with the quill and the inkwell,' you wouldn't have liked it." Shenker's fingers were still in motion:

> What hath overwrought God?

On the way back to *The New Yorker*, I stopped at a phone booth, coupled my ear to the earpiece, and dialed 556-1330. After a moment came a clear, piercing response in high C sharp—the sort of thing only German shepherds are supposed to be able to hear. Since I was not a cassette, there was nothing I could say. The phone, held close to the ear, caused pain.

EYES STARE OUT of the darkness, green and narrow. They move closer. A young black cat, just full grown, steps out of a bit of sewer pipe and starts to move through the city. Its gait is stealthy, preying. It walks across curbs and over the cracks in sidewalks. It hunts and bristles and pads along, looking. The eyes again. Another cat. Snarl. Fangs. Battle. A fierce toss of bodies, fearsome screeches, victory. The black cat moves on. All the while, words are appearing above, below, beside the animal. And people's names. Directed by Edward Dmytryk. Titles designed by Saul Bass. Charles K. Feldman presents *Walk on the Wild Side.*

"Titles designed by Saul Bass" is the arresting line. Movie audiences used to resent, with the same resentment that is provoked by a television commercial, the long parade of credits at the beginning of a film. Saul Bass has single-handedly changed that. More than half of New York's film critics actually cited Bass's black stalking malkin as far and away the best thing in *Walk on the Wild Side.* It was. Suggesting the story's themes, it set a mood that the ensuing picture tried but failed to match.

Bass is imitated by just about everybody now, but no one has come near him. Sometimes his effects are relatively simple. Looking up from the hub of a wagon wheel, he stared out across a tan Pacific of endless real estate and then placed three small words on the threshold of infinity: *The Big Country.* To credit the cast and crew of *The Seven Year Itch*, he used a set of pastel panels opening like tessellated greeting cards. That was all. But the colors and layout were as visually delightful as a Mondrian in motion. And the "t" in *Itch* scratched itself.

TOM EGLIN'S SENSE OF HUMOR, sharp enough in the first place, seemed to rise—to become increasingly rich in perception and range—in response to his besetting illness. Wry, funny, anecdotal, he was an easy patient to visit. He cheered *you* up. He told *you* stories. There was a basketball backboard in his bedroom with a berserk little ball. He counted up, with amusement, the shots you missed.

Mindful of our common Scottish backgrounds—his even closer in time than mine—he told me a story about taking his sons on a voyage among the isles of Scotland. An educational cruise it was, professors aboard, a ship called *Argonaut*, a captain who was not called Jason. As the boys sailed into the very waters of their heritage, they were seasick. This, as they had read, was

> the land of the bens and the glens, where not even
> Sir Walter Scott could exaggerate the romantic
> beauty of that lake and mountain country penetrated
> by fjords that came in from seas that were starred
> with islands. The weather changes so abruptly
> there—closing in, lifting, closing in again—that all in
> an hour wind-driven rain may be followed by calm and
> hazy sunshine, which may then be lost in heavy mists
> that soon disappear into open skies over dark-blue seas.
> When the ocean is blue, the air is as pure as a lens, and

the islands seem imminent and almost encroaching, although they are ten or fifteen miles away—Mull, for example, Scarba, Islay, Jura, the Isles of the Sea.

With all that off the starboard rail, the boys were seasick; and when they were finished being seasick, they came down with flu and went into steerage in the hold. Telling the story with a slight blush and smile, Tom confessed annoyance. He said that he had been, in fact, profoundly irritated by his sons' becoming sick, "because the trip, as you can imagine, was not inexpensive." This was one Scottish father speaking to another directly from the heart.

When Bill Bradley came to Princeton, Tom was his freshman adviser, Tom's mission being to guide this aimless youth toward some sort of utilitarian destiny. Evidently, Tom succeeded. It was the beginning of an enduring friendship, and Tom's encouragement and generosity of counsel were prized by Bill from then to now. From time to time, our three paths crossed. When Bill was in college, and practicing by himself one summer in the Lawrenceville field house, he missed six jump shots in a row. He said to us, "You want to know something? That basket is about an inch and a half low." Some days later, Tom got a stepladder, and he and I measured the basket. It was one and three-eighths inches too low. Any basketball player would know that the hoop was low, but not—within an eighth of an inch—how low.

When Bill was an N.B.A. basketball player, in the early nineteen-seventies, he occasionally went to Lawrenceville to practice alone. One day, feeding the ball back to him, I developed a grandiose fantasy. "Suppose I were somehow to get into a game with you in Madison Square Garden," I said. "Could you get *me* a shot in the N.B.A.?" "Of course," he said, and he sketched out a certain baseline move by which a person two feet tall could score on Abdul-Jabbar. At that moment, out of nowhere, Tom appeared. Bradley told him to guard me, and the play worked. Tom and I reversed roles, and the play worked—the play being so ambiguous that I couldn't stop it even though I knew what was going to happen. Now two people whose height added up to a single basketball player's would forever be grateful to Bill for their one and only shot in the N.B.A.

Those are just a couple of reminiscences from one person who first knew Tom in college and later was his frequent tennis partner for ten or fifteen years, including a time when I most especially needed a friend, and in his quiet way, without a great deal actually said, he was right there. Comparable streams of remembrance surround each one of us at this time, all as different and particular as they would be analogous, all relating to this bright figure of quiet humor—this athlete, counselor, teacher—whose capacity for love and friendship were outsize.

ONE AFTERNOON IN 1961, a young actor named Louis Morelli walked into an office in Hollywood. When he walked out, his name was Trax Colton. No one had ever heard of him before, and no one has heard of him since. But he has at least taken his minor place in an ancient rite of Hollywood. Moreover, Morelli was restyled by one of the wizard name changers now practicing the craft—the agent Henry Willson, who turned Marilyn Louis into Rhonda Fleming, Francis McGowan into Rory Calhoun, Arthur Gelien into Tab Hunter, Robert Moseley into Guy Madison, and, his great mind wandering from the New Jersey Palisades to the Strait of Gibraltar, Roy Fitzgerald into Rock Hudson.

Since it is axiomatic in show business that the name is rewritten before the teeth are capped, hundreds of literary types like Willson have, over the years, flung into the air a confetti storm of phony names that have settled lightly but meaningfully on the American culture.

Greatest in number are the Readily Understandables. Issur Danielovitch lacks euphony, so the name was shortened to Kirk Douglas. It is also understandable why Tula Ellice Finklea would want to change her name to Cyd Charisse, Frances Gumm to Judy Garland, Bernie Schwartz to Tony Curtis, Sarah Jane Fulks to Jane Wyman, Emma Matzo to Lizabeth Scott, Judith Tuvim to Judy Holliday, Doris Kappelhoff to Doris Day, Aaron Chwatt to Red Buttons, Zelma Hedrick to Kathryn Grayson, Eunice Quedens to Eve Arden, Natasha Gurdin to Natalie Wood, Barney Zanville to Dane Clark, and William Beedle to William Holden. England's James Stewart, eclipsed by Hollywood's James Stewart, changed his name to Stewart Granger. Frederick Bickel—rhymes with pickle—changed his name to Fredric March. Frederick Austerlitz was just too hobnailed a surname to weight the light soles of Fred Astaire. Cary Grant, of course, would have been unstoppable with any name from Pinky Fauntleroy to Adolf Schicklgruber—even, for that matter, with his own name: Archie Leach.

But the whys start colliding with the wherefores. There is a group, for example, that could be called the Inexplicables. Why would someone with a graceful name like Harriette Lake want to change it to Ann Sothern? John F. Sullivan could have hardly been afraid of being mistaken for John L. when he changed his name to Fred Allen. The name Edythe Marrener is at least as interesting as Susan Hayward. Why change Thelma Ford to Shirley Booth, Jeanette Morrison to Janet Leigh, Edward Flanagan to Dennis O'Keefe, Patricia Beth Reid to Kim Stanley, Virginia McMath to Ginger Rogers, Julia Wells to Julie Andrews, Helen Beck to Sally Rand, Phylis Isley to Jennifer Jones?

Actors with plain, pronounceable, American Legion sort of names yearn for toning up. Ruby Stevens is Barbara Stanwyck; Margaret Middleton is Yvonne De Carlo; Norma Jeane Baker is Marilyn Monroe. Even Gladys Smith found a little more stature in the name Mary Pickford. On the other hand, embarrassed blue bloods shed their hyphens and thus declare their essential homogeneity with the masses. Reginald Truscott-Jones was too obviously soaked in tallyho. He became Ray Milland. Spangler Arlington Brugh denuded himself of all his nominal raiment and emerged as Robert Taylor.

Some real names are out of character. Roy Rogers was Leonard Slye. Boris Karloff could not have frightened a soul as William Henry Pratt. Gypsy Rose Lee has done things that Rose Louise Hovick would presumably never do. Other real names seem to be struggling to express themselves. Merry Mickey Rooney was once Joseph Yule Jr. Sam Goldwyn was Samuel Goldfish. Shelley Winters was Shirley Schrift; Lili St. Cyr was Willis Marie Van Schaack; Diana Dors was Diana Fluck.

Hollywood stars come from every sort of ethnic and national-origin minority group. Many of them are bitterly vocal about democracy's failures. If enough of them had stuck by their original names, the resulting influence, through the vast popularity of the movies, would have done much to soften bias and reduce prejudice. No one would challenge their actions individually, but they could have served themselves better as a group.

Among actors of Italian and Spanish background, for example, Dino Crocetti opted to be Dean Martin, Margarita Cansino became Rita Hayworth, Anna Maria Louisa Italiano is now Anne Bancroft. Anglicizing their names, Anthony Benedetto became Tony Bennett and Giovanni de Simone became Johnny Desmond. Among Jews, Izzy Itzkowitz probably needed to sandpaper that a bit, yet he stayed with a Jewish name: Eddie Cantor. But most—from Jerry Levitch (Jerry Lewis) to Nathan Birnbaum (George Burns), Emanuel Goldenberg (Edward G. Robinson), Pauline Levy (Paulette Goddard), Rosetta Jacobs (Piper Laurie), and Melvyn Hesselberg (Melvyn Douglas)—have preferred the Anglo-Saxon angle.

Many actors sculpt their real names. Ethel Zimmerman clipped off the zim. Vivien Hartley lost her hart. James Baumgarner dropped the baum. Grace Stansfield is now Gracie Fields. Milton Berle was once Mendel Berlinger. One letter made the difference for Dorothy Lambour. First names have a habit of turning into surnames. Benny Kubelsky changed his name to Jack Benny, Muni Weisenfreund to Paul Muni.

Last names vanish: Arlene Francis Kazanjian, Eddie Albert Heimberger. Some stars can't stand their first names—for example, Leslie Hope and Harry Crosby.

Lolita Dolores Martinez Asunsolo Lopez Negrette is now Dolores Del Rio. Marion Morrison probably thought his name sounded girlish so he changed it to John Wayne. Douglas Fairbanks was really Douglas Ulman. June Allyson was Ella Geisman. Estelle Merle O'Brien Thompson, of Tasmania, started her career as Queenie Thompson, outgrew that, and became Merle Oberon. Yul Brynner goes around saying that his original name was Taidje Khan Jr., and that it derives from northeast Asia, but he is probably Joseph Doaks or something close to that. No one has ever been able to pin him down about his background, not even his wives.

Meanwhile, Rip Torn, that bisyllabic symbol of absurdly phony Hollywood names, is really Rip Torn. His father was Rip Torn, too.

MANY OF THEM WERE KIDS, nineteen or twenty years old, often newly married, with a couple of yoke of oxen and no fear at all. On a good day, they could make fourteen miles, and after two months of walking or jolting along they still had fifteen hundred to go. When a baby was born, the wagon train would stop for a few hours. They were not the sort of people to die on the trail, and amazingly few did. In fact, the skeletons that are strewn all over the emigrants' path in George R. Stewart's *The California Trail* are almost entirely the remains of oxen, milch cows, and Hollywood scriptwriters. Indians, Stewart says, "were a minor nuisance, not a real hazard." A wagon trail to California was first attempted in 1841, and new tries were made each year, but no white traveller was killed by an Indian until 1845.

Later, when the Indians did strike from time to time, there is no record anywhere that they galloped around in circles twanging arrows into the ring of wagons, an absolutely pointless maneuver since the Indians would have been exposing themselves to rifle fire from protected riflemen. Instead, they laid siege, taking command of any springs or streams, until the white men's tongues turned black. But that was rare.

No one used Conestoga wagons: they were too ungainly. Smaller ones, with boxes about nine feet by four feet, were popular. They were not called prairie schooners. When deep rivers were encountered, the bottoms of the boxes could be covered with canvas or hides. Off came the wheels and the vehicle became a boat. On land, they were pulled by oxen or mules. An ox cost twenty-five dollars, a mule seventy-five. No horses. Too weak.

While they were still in the relative East, they ate three-star meals, with hot biscuits, fresh butter, honey, milk, cream, venison, wild peas, tea, and coffee all included in a single typical dinner. Toward the other end, they ate rancid bacon, mountain sheep, red fox, and sometimes boiled hides. When they were dying of thirst, they drank mule urine. While forty-seven of the eighty-seven members of the Donner Party were dying of hunger in 1846, there was some cannibalism. "What do you think I cooked this morning?" said Aunt Betsy Donner one day. "Shoemaker's arm."

SNOW. I WENT INTO THE CITY in the nineteen-forties to see Bud Palmer drop the long one-hander from the Ninth Avenue and Fiftieth corner of Madison Square Garden, and got up in the morning in a friend's apartment to look down on white blisters of cars completely buried in snow. I remember snow in the city in the nineteen-fifties so deep that nothing but pedestrians moved. During another blizzard of the fifties—a storm so effective that it shut down every airport, railroad, and major highway in the Middle Atlantic and northeastern states—the sentinel blimps of the United States Navy were the only means of transportation able to move, and they were transporting nobody; they were out over the North Atlantic to alert us to surprise attacks.

At home in New Jersey, I have been snowed in for as much as three days, but that has less to do with record storms than it has to do with New Jersey's record. In the eighties, my wife and I spent a night in New York and returned to find our car up to its headlights in snow in the Princeton Junction parking lot. Principal roads were plowed. We took a taxi to a sporting-goods store, where, as it happened, we had some days earlier put in an order for cross-country boots and skis. We picked them up while the taxi waited, and it took us to the head of our road, which, as we had imagined, was under three feet of snow, un-plowed. Dressed for the theatre, we skied the mile home.

In the seventies, I spent a February and part of March near the Arctic Circle in Alaska, where winter lacks the savagery it can loose on New York. The dry cold of the Alaskan interior doesn't bite as hard, even at low temperature, as a stiff bitter wind in Times Square. The air is so still for so long in Alaska that snow in light loaves on the spruce boughs can be destroyed completely with a smaller puff of breath than would blow out a candle.

Records are where you find them, and for me—now come up here by the stove, daughters, while I finish this story—my deepest snow was not in New York and not in Alaska but in Benson, Minnesota. In March, 1965, I was riding the Empire Builder, of the old Great Northern Railway, out of Chicago for

Portland because in those days I was afraid to fly. Those days ended near Benson, where the train, which for a hundred miles had ground valiantly into deepening whiteness, was stopped—you guessed it—cold. The snow outside the windows was higher than the train. Eventually we would learn that this was one of the greatest snowstorms in the history of Minnesota. Some hours after the heating system failed, the train crew built fires on the steel plates between cars. It didn't matter that the doors were open. The cold within had matched the cold without, and all along the train—like some sort of encampment—the fires burned above the couplings. We warmed ourselves there by turns, and went back to our frigid seats. We ate warm meals in the ice-cold dining car. Enough booze to build an empire was offered freely to all. Gradually, a snow remover worked its way south to rescue us, sucking up and blowing away its own small blizzard, its advance expressible in feet per hour. It reached us the next day, and at last we moved slowly forward, between high walls of snow that threatened to cave in on the train. The snow in Benson was deeper than roofs, and whole neighborhoods were all but hidden, the houses of Minnesota like the cars of New York—just rows of blisters under snow.

HE WAS A TALL MAN of swift humor whose generally instant responses reached far into memory and wide for analogy. Not much missed the attention of his remarkably luminous and steady eyes. He carried with him an education from the Boston Latin School, Phillips Exeter Academy, Harvard College—

and a full year under the sky with no shelter as an infantryman in France in the Second World War. Arriving there in a landing craft, he forgot his rifle and left it on the boat.

Gore Vidal, a friend of his since Exeter, once asked him why he had given up work as a reporter in order to become an editor.

Robert Bingham said, "I decided that I would rather be a first-rate editor than a second-rate writer."

The novelist drew himself up indignantly, saying, "And what is the matter with a second-rate writer?"

Nothing, of course. But it is given to few people to be a Robert Bingham.

For nearly twenty years he was a part of *The New Yorker*, primarily as an editor of factual writing. In that time, he addressed millions of words with individual attention, giving each a whisk on the shoulders before sending it into print. He worked closely with many writers and, by their testimony, he may have been the most resonant sounding board any sounder ever had. Adroit as he was in reacting to sentences before him, most of his practice was a subtle form of catalysis done before he saw a manuscript.

Talking on the telephone with a writer in the slough of despond, he would say, "Come, now, it can't be that bad. Nothing could be that bad. Why don't you try it on me?"

"But you don't have time to listen to it."

"We'll make time. I'll call you back after I finish this proof."

"Will you?"

"Certainly."

In the winter and spring of 1970, I read sixty thousand words to him over the telephone.

If you were in his presence, he could edit with the corners of his mouth. Just by angling them down a bit, he could suggest deleting something. On and off, he had a mustache. When he had a mustache, he was a little less effective with that method of editing, but effective nonetheless.

As an editor, he wanted to keep his tabula rasa. He was mindful of his presence between writer and reader, and he wished to remain invisible while representing each. He deliberately made no move to join the journeys of research. His writers travelled to interesting places. He might have gone, too. But he never did, because he would not have been able to see the written story from a reader's point of view.

Frequently, he wrote me the same note. The note said, "Mr. McPhee, my patience is not inexhaustible." But his patience *was* inexhaustible. When a piece was going to press, he stayed long into the evening while I fumbled with prose under correction. He had pointed out some unarguable flaw. The fabric of the writing needed reweaving, and I was trying to do it in a way satisfactory to him and to the over-all story. He waited because he respected the fact that the writing had taken as much as five months, or even five years, and now he was giving this or that part of it just another five minutes.

Edmund Wilson once said that a writer can sometimes be made effective "only by the intervention of one who is guileless enough and human enough to treat him, not as a monster, nor yet as a mere magical property which is wanted for accomplishing some end, but simply as another man, whose sufferings elicit his sympathy and whose courage and pride he admires." When writers are said to be gifted, possibly such intervention has been the foremost of the gifts.

I REMEMBER BEING SURPRISED by how green it was. When I first went up to Alaska in summer, I found T-shirt weather in the Brooks Range, beyond the Arctic Circle. If a cloud crossed the sun, of course, you reached for a sweater, but there was, with it all, an unexpected Alaska.

That fall, a bald young man with a handlebar mustache told me that when he had left Chicago to live in Alaska, someone had asked him why he was going. His response had been, "If you have to ask that question you wouldn't understand the answer." I was still near the beginnings of sensing what he meant. While going down a river in Arctic Alaska, I had come to feel what was for me the new perspective of being hundreds of miles from the nearest highway, and I was more than beginning to sense that this terrain could not even roughly be comprehended if it were looked upon as an extension of anything I had known before. Within the mind (as on the ground) I had a long way to go. The fifty-five-gallon steel drums, Blazo cans, old bedsprings, and assorted detritus lying around the cabins of bush villages were still as unappealing to me as they had been when I had first seen them. I was from the megalopolitan towns, where bulldozers bury that sort of thing. In some places in my part of the world, people are so numerous that if they were all to come out of the buildings at once they would not fit in the streets. As one result, and perhaps as a form of survival, they tend to close each other out. Conversation goes off at peculiar angles. Glances run perpendicular to the channel of the talk. No one is listening. In the small, high-latitude communities—towns of nineteen people, towns of nine, of ninety—a human being is an event. An individual is like a book arriving in the mail. Ask a hundred people why they came to Alaska. Aside from the general fact that for one reason or another they wanted to get away from what they call "the Lower Forty-eight," a distillate answer is, "I wanted to be in a place where an individual counts." After some more time there, the Blazo cans and the bunk springs begin to look positively attractive. With regard to the steel barrels, it is not just with irony that they are called the state flower. When you have been looking at them long enough, they bloom.

I once went down to Anchorage at the end of a long stay in various places in eastern interior Alaska, and almost immediately was drawn into a white-water canoe race on a creek that runs through the bowl of Anchorage after dropping from the Chugach Mountains. We raced six miles, dodging boulders and old earthmover tires, and came to the finish among a group of spectators who were drinking Coke and beer. By almost anyone's standards, it was a small crowd—some dozens of people on a riverbank. What occurred to me, though, as we plowed into a gravel bar to end the race, was that there were more people by far in that small assemblage than the total number of people I had encountered—Indians, whites, itinerant miscellany—over the past several months in forty thousand square miles of the upper Yukon valley. A day or two later I was in New Jersey, walking around with such a sense of disorientation that I was bewildered and had an erratic impulse to cry out. Leaves on twigs looked like baseball gloves. The university, in the town where I live, made sense somehow, but almost nothing else made any sense at all here in the world's premier corridor of transportation and commerce. I could feel myself turning from a three-dimensional picture back into the old two-dimensional negative. I got beyond it, of course, but not over it. A Brooks Range guide, who had come east to testify in Washington, stopped at my house one time and I told him I was not sure of what I was trying to express but I felt guilty, somehow, that I was not in Alaska. He said he knew just what I meant, because he felt guilty, too; and in the morning he went back to Alaska. I followed, and followed again. You go out to Chicago and get off the feeder line and start walking for Northwest 3. That is the airplane that lugs all the people from eastern America who want to go to Alaska. You walk a long way to get to it—up to half a mile and more, past every airline known to the mid-continent and on through long empty corridors; and after tens of hundreds of yards you notice that the people around you are thinning out. You press on, and eventually come into an oval bay of ticket counters below a frieze of the names of airlines—Lufthansa, Air France, Swiss Air, SAS, Aer Lingus—and you keep on going. You enter more corridors, void now of people, and you hike on to the remotest working face of O'Hare. There, at last, you find a small cluster of people in wool shirts and down vests. You have hiked your way out of the United States and into the nut of Alaska.

Alaska seems to twang some atavistic American chord, offering remembrance of the earlier frontiers and, heaven knows, engendering in people of the Lower Forty-eight some admiring envy of the people up there. To become absorbed in an almost total way with a people and a place and then suddenly to be cut off from those people, except through the mail, is something that could be listed among the liabilities of the writing life. One February evening, I took a long walk on the frozen Yukon, knowing it was the last night that I would be there. The sun was disappearing, and there were pink bolts across a blue sky above the white river. The big stars came out quickly. And I said to myself, "So long. This is it. The mail plane comes tomorrow and you've had it now."